INSIGHT COMPACT GUIDE

EDINBURGH

GREAT LITTLE GUIDES

Compact Guide: Edinburgh is the perfect quick-reference guide to Scotland's capital. From its magnificent castle to its quaint alleys, from the wealth of its museums to the liveliness of its pubs, everything you need to know about the city is clearly set out in these pages.

This is one of more than 100 titles in Insight Guides' series of pocket-sized, easy-to-use guidebooks edited for the independent-minded traveller. Compact Guides are in essence travel encyclopedias in miniature, designed to be comprehensive yet portable, as well as up-to-date and authoritative.

Star Attractions

An instant reference to some of Edinburgh's most popular tourist attractions to help you on your way.

Edinburgh Castle p16

St Giles' Kirk p20

Royal Museum p27

Princes Street p31

National Gallery of Scotland p32

Georgian House p34

Water of Leith Walkway p38

Forth Railway Bridge p49

Burns in Leith p45

The coast p50

Rosslyn Chapel p57

EDINBURGH

Introduction

Places

Culture

Leisure

Practical Information

Edinburgh – A Tale of Two Cities

Opposite: The Edinburgh Military Tattoo

Fiction could have been kinder to Edinburgh. Robert Louis Stevenson, a native of the city, based *Dr Jekyll and Mr Hyde* on a notorious local murderer, and many have extended this parable of the divided mind to the city itself, contrasting its Calvinistic gentility with its low-life drug scene. Muriel Spark's Miss Jean Brodie simultaneously preached the virtues of self-discovery and extolled the merits of Italian fascism. And in dozens of movies from *Dr No* onwards, Sean Connery has deployed the world's most celebrated Edinburgh accent to conjure up a potent mixture of charm and threat.

Morton's Coat of Arms, Edinburgh Castle

Such ambivalance towards their capital and its character is most likely to emanate from the Scots themselves, a critical people. First-time visitors will more probably agree with Thomas Jefferson, America's third president, who described Edinburgh as a city 'that no place in the world can pretend to equal'. He was referring specifically to Edinburgh's New Town, completed between 1767 and 1830. In this area of approximately one square mile are located 10,000 buildings listed for their architectural merit, many of them still in private residential use.

Edinburgh also has a remarkable medieval town which sprang up around and along the spine of rock which has held a castle on its summit since humans first needed to defend themselves. In 1513 the Flodden Wall was thrown up as protection against an English invasion which failed to materialise. Walls gave protection, but they also crushed a growing population too closely together, with all levels of society forced to live cheek by jowl in a complex of overcrowded vertical tenements. By the 18th century it was time to expand, and that expansion took the form of the largest Georgian city development ever conceived. To this has been added Victorian and modern building, creating a distinctive and attractive skyline.

The town in the 16th century

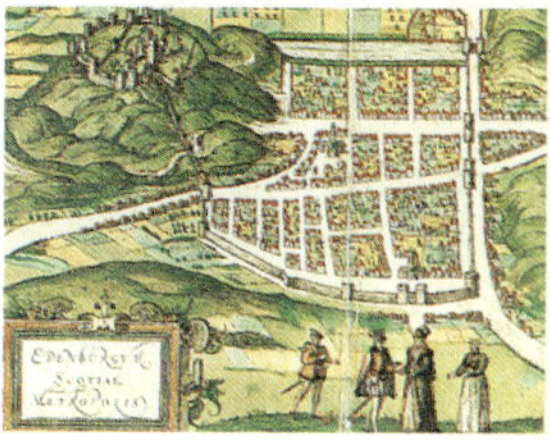

Much else has changed. A century ago the city was known as Auld Reekie (Old Smokey) as a result of the noxious pall created by peat and coal smoke from the many chimneys in the Royal Mile. Now its centre has been awarded World Heritage Site status by UNESCO.

On guard at the Castle

Edinburgh combines a famous castle and many monuments with narrow streets and broad boulevards. It offers spectacular art treasures, sporting and athletic diversions, and a year-round theatre, music and dance programme which culminates each August in the world's largest three-week cultural festival. For three days over the New Year, it becomes the Hogmanay Capital of the World with a carnival, side-shows and concerts. *Auld Lang Syne* is endlessly sung, resonant with fellowship and humanity. This is the capital of a country with a strong sense of identity.

Location and Size

Strategically situated inland from the southern shore of the Firth of Forth, an estuary of the North Sea on Scotland's east coast, the capital has sprawled outwards in every direction. Like Rome, the city is built on seven hills. Rising above Princes Street, the main shopping promenade, is the castle rock, a volcanic plug where the first defensive settlement was founded over 2,000 years ago, and a landmark to anyone who is lost.

To the south, around and below, is the Old Town, sloping east along the Royal Mile, beyond the Flodden Wall and towards the parkland of Holyrood. To the north, between the castle and the Port of Leith on the Firth of Forth, sprawls the New Town, which dates from the late 18th century.

Edinburgh has 441,620 inhabitants, although this number trebles during the summer months when the city becomes Britain's second most popular tourist destination. With the University of Edinburgh established in 1583, Edinburgh College of Art in 1909, Napier College of Science and Technology in 1964 (now Napier University), and Heriot-Watt University in 1966, there has always been a significant student population.

Sunbathing by the Scott Monument

The Climate

The weather on Scotland's east coast is drier and fresher than on the west, but Edinburgh is notorious for the seasonal North Sea 'haar', a mist which periodically settles over the city like a grey blanket.

Generally, however, summers are warm, although often cloudy, and winters are cold but clear. On balmy summer evenings a notable feature is the smell of malt wafting across the city from the Scottish & Newcastle Brewery at Fountainbridge and the North British Distillery at Gorgie.

Piper on parade

The People

The citizens of Edinburgh have a reputation for being reserved and somewhat prim. There's a saying that while 'breeding' in Glasgow, Scotland's competing city on the west coast, is thought of as good fun, 'breeding' in Edinburgh is considered good form. A variant is the Glaswegian accusation that Edinburgh women are 'all fur coats and nae drawers [*no underwear*]'. These jibes don't so much indicate any objective truth as underline the lasting rivalry between the two cities.

The Edinburgh view is that the jealousy grew out of the city's 19th-century boom in middle-class clerical jobs in banking and insurance, which contrasted with Glasgow's reliance on heavy industry such as shipbuilding. It may date back even further. It's possible that the people's ingrained restraint sprung to some extent from the Protestant religion which has dominated lowland Scotland from the 17th century.

Whereas Glaswegians, in general, reflect a vibrant Irish/Celtic west coast origin, Edinburgh evolved long before from Pictish, Saxon and Norman influences. The original Scots, a Celtic people from Ireland, had arrived on the islands and mainland of the west coast to form their separate kingdom of Dalriada. From the 6th century until Kenneth I, the 36th King of Dalriada, merged the two kingdoms, they systematically overwhelmed and integrated with the resident Pict community. In the 11th century, Saxons, fleeing from William the Conqueror, who had subjugated England, began to arrive on the Scottish border, and in 1124 David I, having grown up at the court of his brother-in-law, Henry I of England, invited many of his Norman friends to accompany him when he returned to Scotland to become king. At the same time there were continual Viking invasions from the north.

By the beginning of the 16th century, Edinburgh was established as Scotland's capital, and a professional class was spawned. A harsh blow to the people's self-esteem was dealt in 1707 by the Act of Union, which united Scotland with England under one monarch and parliament – based, of course, 400 miles away in London. Scotland retained its own Church and legislature, but the feeling that Edinburgh had become a hollow capital persisted to the late 20th century, until the new Labour Government in Britain finally granted Scotland its own parliament again (*see page 8*).

But, although political power ebbed away from Edinburgh following the Act of Union, intellectual influence did not. Towards the end of the 18th century, well into the 1830s and over a period which became known as the Scottish Enlightenment, the city drew together some of the most stimulating minds in Europe.

In a tavern off the Royal Mile, David Hume, who wrote a six-volume history of England, would hold court with the physician William Cullen, the chemist Joseph Black, the mathematician John Playfair, the dramatist John Home, the first sociologist Adam Fergusson, and the first economist Adam Smith. For an all-too brief moment, the poet Robert Burns flirted with the Edinburgh salons of 'Clarinda', his sponsor, the wealthy Mrs MacLehose, and towards the end of this golden age Sir Walter Scott's novels had become best-sellers throughout Europe. Painters of the calibre of Henry Raeburn, Allan Ramsay, Jr, and David Wilkie documented the age, while the Adam family dazzled the nation with architectural achievement. It was Edinburgh's finest hour.

King Robert the Bruce gives the city its charter in 1329

History in pub signs: James VI and Mary Queen of Scots

A drink is never far away

The city derives much of its character from that era of grace and elegance, although Calvinist doctrines encouraged a tension to develop between professional and artistic pursuits. But enjoyment is not always chained to restraint. Although Edinburgh's nightlife, outside of the festival period, could hardly be described as spectacular, there are plenty of intimate bars and restaurants where conviviality reigns. And, given the city's strong student population, there are plenty of nightclubs eager to cater for a younger clientele.

With a heavily residential city centre, Edinburgh is unlike other British cities, although socially it can be as clique-ridden as anywhere else. The juxtaposition of social classes in close proximity to each other possibly contributes to a surface formality, but beneath is a generous personality.

The city's prim image was decisively shattered when, in the late 1980s, Edinburgh was dubbed the Aids capital of Europe. The high per capita incidence of HIV owed less to sexual practices than to the sociable habit of needle-sharing among drug users, although the provision of clean needles did much to control the spread of the epidemic. The city's reputation for drug abuse has proved hard to live down, however, particularly given the popularity of such cult films as *Trainspotting*.

Easy-going Edinburgh

For most of the year it is Edinburgh's climate that makes for more of an indoor, than outdoor, existence, and locals, for the most part, tend to go about their everyday lives immune to the weather. When the sun does come out, however, the city is transformed, somewhat absurdly, with tourist and office worker alike taking full advantage of the many green spaces for sunbathing.

The Government

The first elections to a Scottish parliament in nearly 300 years were held on 6 May 1999, after a referendum had confirmed the people's wish to self-govern. Donald Dewar now heads a 'home rule' Government based in Edinburgh.

The Economy

Edinburgh is a financial centre of international standing, founded on traditional virtues of prudence and propriety, combined with a flair for innovation. Furthermore, the financial services sector embraces banking, insurance and pensions, and Scotland now ranks third in the European Union for specialist fund management. This eminence shouldn't surprise: it was a Scotsman, after all (William Paterson), who founded the Bank of England in 1694. And it was Adam Smith, born in Kirkcaldy, a small fishing village near Edinburgh, who produced the 1776 masterwork

Retailers depend on tourists

Fun below the Castle

The Wealth of Nations, championing the paradox of private gain yielding public good.

Edinburgh lawyers and accountants took Smith's doctrines seriously. In the late 19th century, they gathered together the surplus funds of Scottish industrialists and made fortunes by investing in such projects as American railroads and the rebuilding of Chicago after the 1871 fire.

Although for most of the 20th century Edinburgh's financial institutions have largely occupied the spacious rooms of the New Town streets between Charlotte Square and St Andrew Square, new technology has influenced an exodus to purpose-built accommodation elsewhere: Saltire Court in Castle Terrace, in close proximity to the rotunda of the Edinburgh International Conference Centre, and the Gyle Business Park, west of the city. In consequence, a number of fine Georgian buildings are now being restored to their former residential glory.

Busking Edinburgh-style

The Law

Scottish Law remained, after 1707, distinctly different from English Law, and this variance, which was guaranteed by the Act of Union, has made an important contribution towards preserving a Scottish identity. Because Scotland broadly follows the Roman Law tradition, Scots tend to be much more in sympathy with European Law than are the English, who follow the English Common Law system.

Terminology differs, too. A litigant is a 'pursuer' and the sued is a 'defender'. If you disagree too outspokenly with a judge's decision, you may be accused of 'murmuring the judge'. Barristers are known as advocates, and the judges of local courts are sheriffs. And there's the useful verdict of 'not proven' which doesn't exist in English law and which is cynically interpreted to mean 'we think the accused did it but we can't prove it'.

The Sheriff Courthouse

Historical Highlights

900BC Bronze Age settlement on Castle Rock.

208BC–12AD Roman fortifications are built at Cramond, on the River Almond, to service the Antonine Wall, the defensive fortification which stretched from the Firth of Forth to the Firth of Clyde, north of modern-day Glasgow.

600 Dun Edein, the fort on the rock, is occupied by Gododdin tribe before falling to the Angles of Northumbria in 638.

843 Kenneth MacAlpin unites the kingdoms of Scots and Picts.

1076 King Malcolm III of Scotland builds a little chapel of worship for his wife, Queen Margaret, on the highest point of Castle Rock. Margaret is canonised by the Pope in 1250.

1125 David I makes Edinburgh a Royal Burgh.

1128 Holyrood Abbey founded by David I for Augustinian monks.

1286 Alexander III, the last Celtic King of Scots, is killed in a riding accident. The throne passes to his three-year-old granddaughter, Princess Margaret of Norway.

1290 Margaret, 'Maid of Norway', dies on a ship off the Orkney Islands during her journey to Scotland to be crowned Queen.

1292 With the approval of Edward I of England, John Balliol, a distant relative to the Royal House of Scotland, is crowned King of Scots at Scone.

1295 Balliol defiantly signs treaty with France.

1296 Edinburgh Castle is captured by Edward I of England. Balliol forced to abdicate.

1297–1304 First War of Independence. Led by William Wallace, the Scots rise up against English domination. A major invasion compels the Scots to negotiate terms but, after the capture and execution of Wallace, many Scots are sufficiently outraged to think again.

1306–28 Second War of Independence. Robert the Bruce, also a claimant to the Scottish throne, renews the struggle against the English.

1313 Edinburgh Castle is besieged and mostly destroyed by Sir Thomas Randolph.

1314 Robert the Bruce wins great victory over the English army of Edward II at Bannockburn and liberates Scotland from English domination.

1328 Treaty of Edinburgh recognising Scotland's independence is signed between Robert I of Scotland and Edward III of England.

1514 Flodden Wall is put up around the city after the Scots are heavily defeated at the Battle of Flodden, in Northumberland. But Henry VIII does not invade as expected.

1544 Determined that the infant Mary Queen of Scots should marry his son, the future Edward VI of England, Henry VIII sends the Earl of Hertford to sack Edinburgh Castle. This is known as The Rough Wooing. Mary is despatched to France for safety, and is betrothed to the Dauphin.

1559 John Knox is appointed Minister of St Giles' Kirk. Mary de Guise, mother of Mary Queen of Scots, as Regent of Scotland, defends Leith against the Protestant Lords of Congregation, who object to her Catholic politics. Eventually she retires to Edinburgh Castle where she dies in 1560.

1560 Treaty of Edinburgh, also called Treaty of Leith, is signed between the French and English recognising the joint sovereignty of Mary and her husband François II of France over Scotland, while acknowledging Elizabeth I as Queen of England.

1561 Mary Queen of Scots, having been briefly Queen of France, returns to Scotland when her husband dies. She astutely gives her official blessing to the Reformed Church of Scotland.

1565 Mary Queen of Scots marries her cousin, Lord Darnley.

1567 Lord Darnley is blown up in a house at Kirk O'Field, beside the Palace of Holyroodhouse. Three months later Mary marries the Earl of Bothwell.

1568 Mary Queen of Scots loses Battle of Langside against her own nobles and flees to England.

1571–73 Edinburgh Castle besieged by the Earl of Moray who is determined to suppress the remaining supporters of Mary Queen of Scots.

1583 Edinburgh University, the first non-ecclesiastical university to be founded in Britain, is opened with 80 students.

1603 On the death of Elizabeth I of England, James VI of Scotland becomes King James I of England, uniting the two thrones.

1638 The National Covenant, a petition objecting to the imposition of Episcopalianism, an English religion, over Scottish Presbyterianism, is signed at Greyfriars.

1643 Solemn League and Covenant agreed between English parliament and Presbyterian Scots.

1645 Edinburgh is ravaged by the plague.

1649 Charles I executed by English Parliament.

1650 Charles II, having agreed to terms of the Covenant, is crowned at Scone. The Palace of Holyroodhouse is occupied by troops commanded by Oliver Cromwell and catches on fire.

1660 Restoration of the monarchy in England and the sovereign in Scotland.

1695 Bank of Scotland is founded in Edinburgh.

1706 In a mass insurrection in protest against the proposed Act of Union, intended to merge the Scottish and English parliaments, a mob attacked the residence of the Lord Provost and took over control of the city until dispersed by the army.

1707 Act of Union passed. Scotland's government moves from Edinburgh to London.

1736 John Porteus, Captain of the Town Guard, is in charge at the public execution of the robber of the Pittenweem Customs House. A riot breaks out during the execution, and Porteus orders his men to fire on the mob. For this he is condemned to death, then reprieved by Queen Caroline. A mob takes the law into its own hands, breaks into the Tolbooth, and hangs Porteus on a dyer's pole in the Grassmarket.

1745 Prince Charles Edward Stuart arrives in Edinburgh with his Highland army, determined to win back the British throne for his father. He wins the Battle of Prestonpans and marches south into England.

1767 Charles Craig wins competition for a plan to build the New Town of Edinburgh.

1772 Last witch to be burned on Castlehill.

1786 Robert Burns publishes the first edition of his Kilmarnock poems and visits Edinburgh, where he receives a rapturous welcome.

1822 Sir Walter Scott organises a celebrated levee at Holyrood Palace for George IV, the first reigning British monarch to set foot on Scottish soil for over 200 years. The Honours of Scotland, the Sword of State, Crown and Sceptre, bricked up within the castle in 1707, are put on show.

1842 Edinburgh is linked to the UK railway network at Waverley and Haymarket.

1844 The Scott Monument is erected.

1890 The Forth Bridge opens, providing a direct rail link with the northeast coast of Scotland.

1947 First Edinburgh International Festival.

1978 Referendum on the re-establishment of a Scottish parliament in Edinburgh is rejected.

1996 Stone of Destiny transferred from Westminster Abbey to Edinburgh Castle.

1997 Labour victory in British General Election leads to another referendum on setting up a Scottish parliament; the people vote 'yes' to domestic self-government with tax-varying powers. Scientists at the Roslin Institute in Edinburgh create Dolly the sheep, the world's first clone of an adult mammal.

1999 First elections to the Scottish parliament are held on 6 May. The Scottish parliament is opened by the Queen on 1 July.

Edinburgh Castle

Route 1

The Grassmarket – Mercat Cross – The Lawnmarket – Camera Obscura – Scotch Whisky Heritage Centre – Edinburgh Castle

Covenanters' memorial

The first route begins at the entrance of the old city and ends with a tour of Edinburgh Castle culminating with a visit to St Margaret's Chapel, the city's oldest building.

★★ **The Grassmarket**, lurking below the south-facing drop of the castle rock, houses trendy boutiques and restaurants, but long ago the monks of the Greyfriars held cattle sales here. On this spot stood the public gallows where executions took place until as late as the 18th century.

The ★ **Covenanters' Memorial** ❶, marking the spot where the common gibbet stood, was erected in 1937, recalling the many martyrs who died for their faith. On West Bow, at the eastern end of this wide space, the roads split off, with the **Cowgate** running east along the lower edge of the Old Town, beneath the high arches of both George IV Bridge and South Bridge. Once a route for cattle on their way to the grazings on the Burgh Muir, the street had become fashionable by the 16th century.

Two streets at West Bow curve up to meet George IV Bridge. Candlemaker Row, sloping uphill from the start of Cowgate, contains the **Hall of the Incorporation of Candlemakers**, built in 1722. Long ago farmers from the north and south would gather together in the inns and taverns of this street. **Victoria Street**, noted for the individuality of its shops, is on the north side of West Bow and curves uphill to connect with the bridge, erected on nine arches by Thomas Hamilton in 1832. The street emerges opposite the ★★ **National Library of Scotland** ❷.

National Library

George IV Bridge leads to the Lawnmarket on the **Royal Mile**, where produce such as wool and linen from 'landward' districts was sold. A complex system of pends, closes, and wynds are found along the full length of the Royal Mile. These provide access to courtyards often named after former inhabitants. **Brodie's Close**, for example, recalls one of the city's more infamous sons, a town councillor and cabinet-maker by day, a burglar by night.

At 447B is **Gladstone's Land ❸** (1 April to 31 October, Monday to Saturday, 10am–5pm; Sunday, 2–5pm), which was the six-storey home of a prosperous Edinburgh merchant in the 17th century. It is decorated and furnished with great authenticity to give an impression of life in Edinburgh's Old Town 300 years ago. ★★ **Lady Stair's House ❹**, named after its owner in the early 18th century, houses a ★ **Writers' Museum** (Monday to Saturday, 10am – 5pm) and incorporates relics belonging to Sir Walter Scott, Robert Burns and Robert Louis Stevenson. Opposite is ★ **Riddle's Court ❺**, built in the 1590s as a residence for Baillie John Macmorran, a wealthy merchant shot dead by a schoolboy during a riot at the Royal High School in 1595. In 1598, a banquet was held here for King James VI and his Queen, Anne of Denmark. The building has a 16th-century painted ceiling and 17th-century plasterwork, and is now an educational centre.

A tenement once said to have been occupied by the Laird o'Cockpen, a 17th-century lord provost of the city, houses the ★★★ **Outlook Tower ❻**, added on by the architect Patrick Geddes in the 19th century. This contains a **Camera Obscura** (daily, April to October, 9.30am–6pm; July and August, late opening; November to March, 10am–5pm). It's an extraordinary, natural cinema providing a live images of the surrounding city, including close-ups of stonemasonry you couldn't otherwise view.

A short distance before the castle esplanade, the road becomes Castlehill, where witches and warlocks were burned from the 16th to 18th centuries, having been first drowned in the Nor' Loch. A short diversion to the left leads to **Ramsay Garden**, a residential complex of privately-owned houses also built by Sir Patrick Geddes to include the homes of that fine Scottish poet Allan Ramsay (1686–1758) and his distinguished painter son, also Allan Ramsay (1713–84).

Follow this steep, cobbled street around the corner for open scenic views over the New Town towards the Firth of Forth, and make a short diversion to the

Gladstone's Land

Celebrating scribes

A room with a view

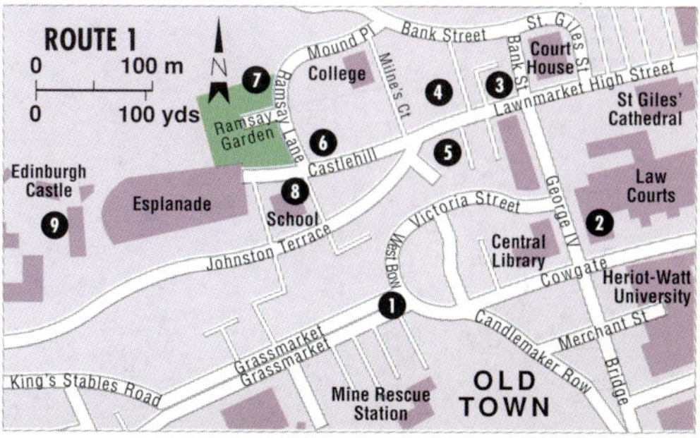

★ **Assembly Hall** ❼, designed by William Playfair to replace a 'palace' occupied by Mary of Guise. Every summer this is the meeting place of the General Assembly of the Church of Scotland, and it is the temporary home of the new Scottish parliament. The building also contains **New College**, for students of theology at Edinburgh University. A suitably austere bronze statue of John Knox holding a bible dominates the quadrangle in front.

Enticing the tourists

At 254, Castle Hill is the ★★★ **Scotch Whisky Heritage Centre** ❽ (daily, June to September 9.30am–6pm; October to May 10am–5pm; closed Christmas Day and New Year's Day). A tour lasting about an hour provides a thorough briefing on Scotch whisky, with a free dram.

The Castle at dusk

Perched high on an extinct volcanic outcrop, ★★★ **Edinburgh Castle** ❾ (April to September 9.30am–6pm, October to March 9.30am–5pm) dominates the city skyline. On the Esplanade each August is held the Edinburgh Military Tattoo, one of the great spectacles of the annual Edinburgh festival season.

Edinburgh Castle has withstood many sieges and occupations in its 1,000-year history. Recent excavations have unearthed evidence of Iron-Age and Dark-Age forts, suggesting the site was occupied as far back as 850 BC.

King Malcolm III and his Saxon Queen Margaret lived here in the 11th century, after which it became a frequent retreat for the medieval Scottish monarchy. After five centuries of attacks by the invading English, it is remarkable that so much of it has survived. From the 12th century onwards, every occupant modified or added to the original structure, so that today it is a rich architectural mix of palace, fortress, barracks, chapel and war memorial.

In the castle courtyard

Enter across the modern **drawbridge** and **gatehouse** [A]. Ahead is the great parapet of the **Half-Moon Battery** [B], built by Regent Morton in 1574 on the ruins of the 14th-century David's Tower. The path then leads towards the **Portcullis Gate** [C], from the same period.

★★★ **The Scottish United Services Museum** [D] is housed in two sites, the first in the Hospital block in the south-east corner, the second in the **Queen Anne Barracks**, Crown Square. Exhibits relate to the history of Scotland's three armed services.

★★ **The Scottish National War Memorial** [E], next door to Queen Anne Barracks, was designed in 1927 by Sir Robert Lorimer, and contains the names of the dead of two world wars.

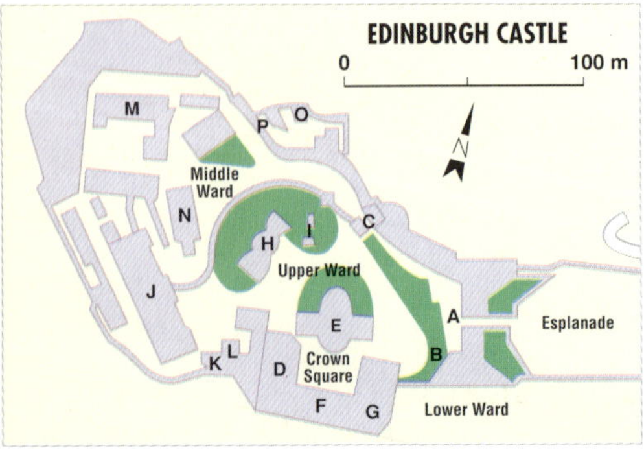

On the south side of the square is the ★ **Great Hall [F]** which dates from the 16th century. Today it is used for ceremonial occasions, dramatised by the hammerbeam ceiling with its ornate carvings.

The Great Hall

Also in the square is the 15th-century **Palace [G]**. In the Royal apartments on the ground floor is **Queen Mary's Room**, where in 1566 Mary Queen of Scots gave birth to the future James VI of Scotland (James I of England).

★★★ **The Crown Room** on the first floor displays the **Honours of Scotland**. The Scottish crown is one of the oldest in Europe, said to date from the reign of Robert I in the 14th century, but with arches from an older crown. The sceptre was a gift from Pope Alexander VI to King James IV in 1494, and the sword of state was a present to that same king by Pope Julius II.

When Oliver Cromwell occupied Scotland in 1651, the Scottish regalia were removed to Dunottar Castle on the Kincardineshire coast, south of Aberdeen, for safe keeping. When Dunottar came under siege, a servant girl smuggled the items out in a flower basket. They lay buried in a churchyard until the Restoration when they were returned to Edinburgh Castle. However, it was not until 1822, when King George IV announced that he was to visit his Scottish subjects, that Sir Walter Scott suggested that the honours be put on display.

Also in the Crown Room is the **Stone of Destiny** (or Stone of Scone), the traditional coronation stone of Scottish monarchs which was stolen by English king Edward I 700 years ago, and finally returned in 1996.

Beside the **reservoir [H]** is the oldest building in the castle, the 12th-century ★★ **St Margaret's Chapel [I]**.

Mons Meg and its 20th-century equivalent

On the left of the **New Barracks [J]** (1796) on the west side of the castle is the **Military Prison [K]** and **Castle Vaults [L]** which contain the castle's most renowned piece of artillery, **Mons Meg**, a cannon employed at the siege of Norham in the 15th century. In the same room is an illustrated exhibition about its manufacture, history and capabilities. On the right of the New Barracks are the **Ordnance Storehouse and Hospital [M]** above the exposed Western Defences. The **Governor's House [N]** in the Middle Ward was built in 1742 as the Castle Governor's official residence, and it now houses the Army Officers' Mess with magnificent views over the city from the Jacobite Dining Room.

One of the best-known features of Edinburgh Castle is the **One O'clock Gun [O]** which is fired from the ramparts every weekday at 1pm. It is said that true natives of Edinburgh, no matter where they are in the world, will always start and look at their watches at one o'clock. The gun is on Mills Mount Battery beside the **Cartshed [P]**, which is now a restaurant.

Kinnear Road
Offices
East Fettes Avenue
Telford College
Newfield Recreation Ground
Inverleith Place
Inverleith B901 Row
Eildon St
Recreation Ground
North Werber Park
INVERLEITH
Arboretum Place
Royal Botanic Garden
Fettes College
Tennis Courts
Inverleith Park
Inverleith Terrace
Western General Hospital
Crewe Road South
Carrington Road
Broughton High School
Arboretum Ave
Glenogle Road
Stockbridge
Brandon St
Craigleith Hill Ave
Lothian & Borders Police HQ
Fettes Avenue
COMELY BANK
North Park
St. Bernard's Row
Coburg St
B900 Henderson Row
Royal Victoria Hospital
CRAIGLEITH
Comely Bank
Comely Bank Rd
Raeburn M
Raeburn Pl
Hamilton Pl
Dundas
Fettes Row
Craigleith B900 Road
Sch
Learmonth Ave
Comely Bank Avenue
Learmonth Gs M
Dean Park St
Dean Street
St. Stephen St
Cumberland
Orchard Bank
Orchard Pl
Orchard Road
Orchard Brae
Comely Grove
St. Bernard's Crescent
Leslie Pl
Dean Terrace
Saunders St
Circus Lane
Royal Circus Pl
Circus
Great King
Howe Street
Northum-
Learmonth Gds
Sth Learmonth Gds
Dean Park Cres
Ann St
India Place
India Street
Orchard Brae Avenue
Learmonth Ter
Lennox St
Doune T
Gloucester La
Queensferry A90 Road
Oxford T
Clarendon Cr
Moray
Heriot Row
Street
Buckingham Terrace
Belgrave Cr La
Eton Ter
Daniel Stewart's and Melville College
Queensferry Terr
Belgrave Pl
Dean Path
Belford Gdns
Belgrave Cres
Place
Queen
Queen Street
N Castle St
Frederick Street
Thistle
Belford Ave
Ravelston Terrace
Dean Village
Ainslie Place
Colme St
Hill St
Young St
Ravelston Dykes
Dean
Bells Brae
Charlotte
Castle St
George Street
Ravelston Pk
Sunbury
Queensferry St
Rose
Street
Whinmill Brae
Scottish National Gallery of Modern Art
Belford Road
Square
Princes A8 Street
Rothesay Pl
Walker
Alva St
Stafford St
Club
Chester St
Melville St
Water of Leith
Douglas Cres
Eglinton Cres
Manor Place
Coates Cres
Shandwick Place
Rutland
Lothian A702 Road
King's Stables Road
Castle Terrace
Coates
Glencairn Cres
Palmerston Place
Atholl Cr
Canning St
Square
Edinburgh Castle
Wester Coates Rd
Wester Coates Ter
Donaldson's School
Magdala Cres
Coates Gdns
Grosvenor Cr
Lansdowne Cr
Atholl Cr La
Canning St
Road
Grindlay St
Lady Lawson St
Theological College
W. Maitland St
Dewar Pl La
Morrison
West Coates A8
Haymarket T
Haymarket
Street
Bread St
Grove
Brewery
Balbirnie Pl
W. Catherine Pl
Devon Pl
West Approach
Gardners Cres
Fountainbridge
High Riggs
Lauriston
Russell
Distillery
Street
Works
Roseburn
Sauchiebank
Works
Duff St
Cathcart Pl
Caledonian Cres
Fountainbridge
Earl Grey St
Home St
Brougham St
Schools
DALRY
Springwell Pl
Fountain Brewery
Works
Road
Downfield Pl
Duff St
West Approach Road
Gilmore Pk
Lochrin Pl
Approach Road
Street
Dundee Street
Fountain Brewery
Union Canal
Gillmore Pl
T.A. Centre
Bowling Greens
Murieston Cr
Dalry A70 Road
Viewforth Works
Place
Schools
Depot
Gibson T
Horne T
Viewforth
Gillespie Cr
Bruntsfield
Dalry Cemetery
Dundee Terrace
Fowler T
Yeaman Pl
Gilmore Place
Leamington Terrace
McLeod
Tay St
Rd
Dorset Pl
Bruntsfield A702
College of Commerce
Bryson Rd
Granville T
Warrender Pk
Cemetery

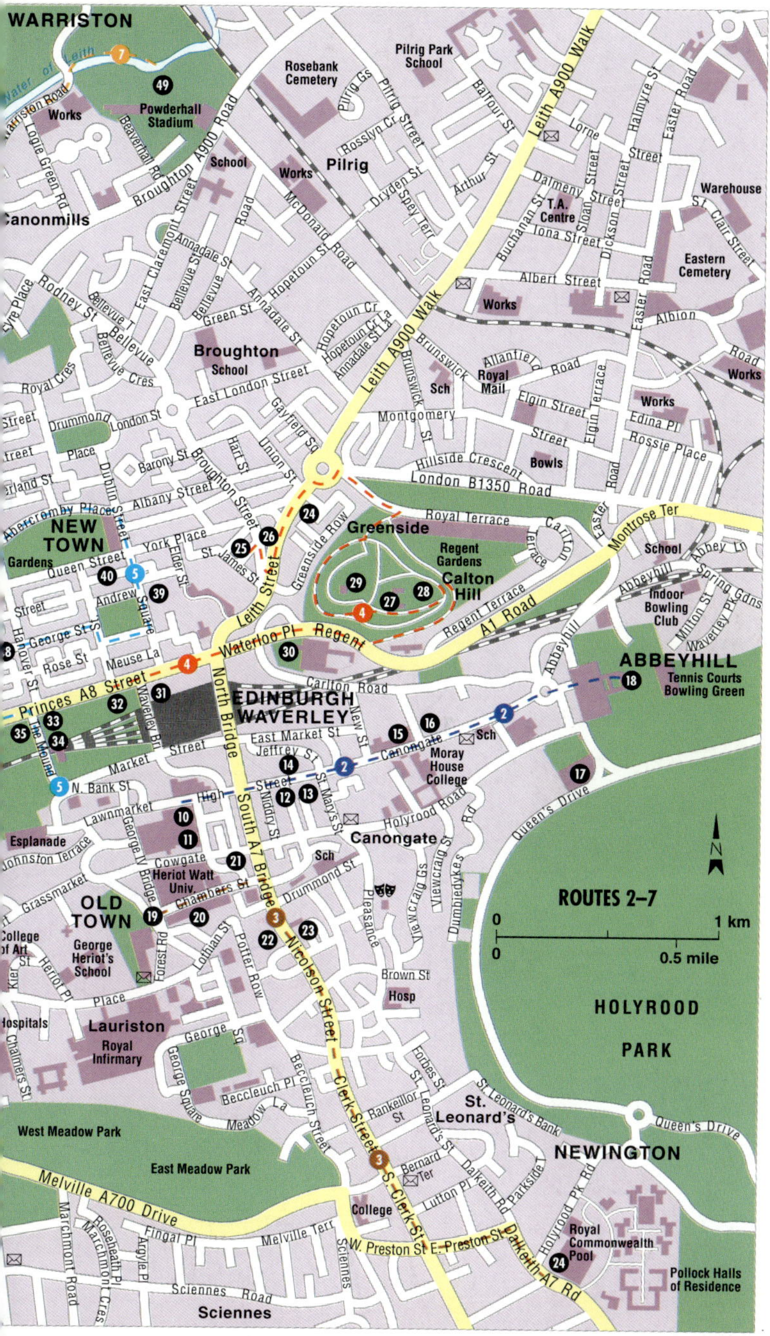
WARRISTON
Water of Leith
Warriston Road
Works
Powderhall Stadium
Beaverhall Rd
Logie Green Rd
Broughton A900 Road
School
Works
Pilrig
Rosebank Cemetery
Pilrig Gs
Pilrig Street
Pilrig Park School
Balfour St
Leith A900 Walk
Rosslyn Cr
Dryden St
Spey Terr
Arthur St
McDonald Road
Canonmills
East Claremont Street
Annandale St
Bellevue St
Bellevue
Hopetoun St
Lorne Street
Halmyre St
Easter Road
Dalmeny Street
T.A. Centre
Buchanan St
Sloan Street
Dickson Street
Iona Street
Warehouse
St. Clair Street
Eastern Cemetery
Albert Street
Works
Easter Road
Albion Road
Works
Rodney St
Bellevue T
Bellevue Cres
Green St
Annandale St
Hopetoun Cr
Hopetoun Cr La
Annandale St La
Brunswick Road
Brunswick St
Allanfield
Royal Mail
Sch
Broughton
School
East London Street
Royal Cres
Drummond Place
London St
Gayfield Sq
Montgomery St
Elgin Street
Elgin Terrace
Works
Edina Pl
Rossie Place
Street
Street
Dublin Street
Barony St
Hart St
Union St
Hillside Crescent
Bowls
London B1350 Road
Albany Street
Broughton Street
Road
Abercromby Place
NEW TOWN
Gardens
York Place
St. James St
Greenside Row
Greenside
Royal Terrace
Carlton Terrace
Easter
Montrose Ter
School
Abbey La
Queen Street
Andrew Square
Elder St
Leith Street
Regent Gardens
Calton Hill
Regent Terrace
A1 Road
Abbeyhill
Spring Gdns
Indoor Bowling Club
Milton St
Waverley Pk
Street
Hanover St
George St
St
Rose St
Meuse La
Waterloo Pl
Regent
Princes A8 Street
Waverley Bri
North Bridge
Carlton Road
EDINBURGH WAVERLEY
ABBEYHILL
Tennis Courts
Bowling Green
The Mound
East Market St
New St
Street
Market
Jeffrey St
Canongate
Sch
Moray House College
N. Bank St
High
Street
Niddry St
St Mary's St
Holyrood Road
Queen's Drive
Lawnmarket
George IV Bridge
South A7 Bridge
Esplanade
Johnston Terrace
Cowgate
Heriot Watt Univ.
Chambers St
Sch
Drummond St
Canongate
Viewcraig St
Viewcraig Gs
Dumbiedykes Rd
Grassmarket
OLD TOWN
Pleasance
ROUTES 2–7
0
1 km
0
0.5 mile
N
College of Art
Kier St
Heriot Pl
George Heriot's School
Forest Rd
Lothian St
Potter Row
Nicolson Street
Brown St
Hosp
HOLYROOD
PARK
Place
Hospitals
Lauriston
Royal Infirmary
Chalmers St
George Sq
George Square
Buccleuch Pl
Buccleuch Street
Meadow La
Clerk Street
Rankeillor St
Forbes St
St. Leonard's St
St. Leonard's
St Leonard's Bank
Queen's Drive
West Meadow Park
East Meadow Park
NEWINGTON
Bernard Ter
Dalkeith Rd
Parkside T
Holyrood Pk Rd
Melville A700 Drive
College
S. Clerk St
Lutton Pl
Royal Commonwealth Pool
Marchmont Road
Rosehall Pl
Marchmont Cres
Argyle Pl
Fingal Pl
Melville Terr
Sciennes
W. Preston St
E. Preston St
Dalkeith A7 Rd
Pollock Halls of Residence
Sciennes Road
Sciennes

High Kirk of St Giles

Route 2

The Royal Mile – The Palace of Holyroodhouse – Holyrood Park – Salisbury Crags – Arthur's Seat *(see map on pages 18–19)*

The route begins at the top of the Old Town and leads along Edinburgh's most commercial tourist street where almost every second shop furnishes tartan and local souvenirs.

The Heart of Midlothian

Charles II forever riding by the High Kirk of St Giles

Much of Scotland's turbulent history was enacted along the **Royal Mile**, a sequence of four streets between Edinburgh Castle and the Palace of Holyrood. Route 1 has covered Castlehill and the Lawnmarket; we can now progress along the High Street and the Canongate.

In front of the entrance to the High Kirk of St Giles is the **Heart of Midlothian**, a heart-shape worked into the cobbles, inspired by the celebrated novel by Sir Walter Scott and signifying the centre of the district in which it stands. A statue of the 5th Duke of Buccleuch, Lord President of the Council in 1846, who built the harbour at Granton, is located nearby. Here stood the **Old** and **New Tollbooths**, the city's administrative centre, and latterly the town jail. As a consequence, the cobbled heart is often spat upon by passers-by. Various legislatures were accommodated in this space and the town curfew would be called at 10pm. The buildings were demolished between 1811 and 1817, and the original tollbooth door was acquired by Sir Walter Scott for use at Abbotsford, the house he built for himself near Melrose.

The ★★★ **High Kirk of St Giles** ❿ (Monday to Saturday 9am–5pm, to 7pm in summer, Sunday 1–6pm) sits on the site of a building erected during the reign of Alexander I (1107–24). This, Scotland's main cathedral, comprises architecture dating from the 12th century. The crown of St Giles is from the 16th century and the spire is supported by eight flying buttresses and topped with a golden weathercock dating from 1567. John Knox, the great Scottish reformer, became its first Protestant minister after the Reformation, and a modern statue of him stands close to the west door. During the reign of Charles II when an attempt was made to introduce the English prayer book, Jenny Geddes, a local housewife, is said to have thrown her folding-stool at the preacher. The consequent uproar helped abolish Episcopacy as the religion of Scotland.

John Knox

Interiors include fine 19th- and 20th-century stained glass, splendid military and civilian memorials, and a very fine organ, designed by Rieger Orgelbau. The West Window is in memory of the poet Robert Burns; the Montrose and Argyll windows bear the arms of the protagonists of the Covenanting period who opposed the enforcement of an English religion on Scotland. The windows in the Moray Aisle depict the funeral of the Regent Moray, Mary Queen of Scots' illegitimate half-brother who was assassinated in Linlithgow.

Queen's Seal, Thistle Chapel

The greatest honour in Scottish life is to be made a Knight of the Thistle, the personal gift of a monarch. It is the equivalent of England's Order of the Garter, and at any one time there are no more than 16 holders. ★★ **The Thistle Chapel**, which sits to the left of the cathedral interior, was a gift from John David, 12th Earl of Leven and 11th Earl of Melville, and designed by Sir Robert Lorimer. Built between 1909 and 1911, it is considered the most ornate post-medieval building of its size in Scotland. The knights' stalls are carved in oak in a light and elegant Gothic style and the original heraldic stall plates were enamelled by Phoebe Traquair.

A shop and a restaurant are situated in the Lower Aisle. For details of times of worship, tel: 0131-225 4363.

From the steps of St Giles, the ★ **Signet Library** stands to the left, adjoining the **Advocates Library** and **Parliament Hall** ⓫ (open to the public), which front onto Parliament Square, behind St Giles. Here the old Scottish parliament met until the 1707 Act of Union brought together Scotland and England. Dating from the Renaissance, the building had a facelift in the early 19th century. Today it provides chambers for the judges of Scotland's Court of Session, advocates and barristers. The hall is 122ft long and 60ft high (37x18 metres), with a 49-ft (15-metre) wide hammerbeam ceiling of dark oak. The stained-glass south windows by Wilhelm von Kaulbach depict the inauguration of the College of Justice by James V. In the square to the east, largely used for parking, is a statue of Charles II on horseback wearing the robes of a Roman emperor.

The Thistle Chapel's ceiling

Detail of the Mercat Cross

The interior of the adjoining Signet Library houses the books of the Society of Writers to H.M. Signet, Scotland's legal fraternity. The vaulted salon of the upper library is often used for concerts and receptions. The ceiling carries Thomas Stotland's 1821 painting of Apollo and the Muses.

On the far side of St Giles' is the ★ **Mercat Cross**, from which proclamations are still made on State occasions. Virtually destroyed in the 18th century, the cross has been admirably restored. The capital and the eight medallions proclaim the royal arms of Britain, Scotland, England and Ireland in company with the arms of Edinburgh, Leith, Canongate and Edinburgh University.

Alexander the Great in action

Immediately across the High Street, through arches, are the ★ **City Chambers**, designed by John Adam but built by John Fergus in the mid-18th century. A statue of Bucephalus being restrained by Alexander, sculpted by Sir John Steell, stands in the forecourt. Beneath the City Chambers are many other buildings on other levels of the original Old Town, notably ★ **Mary King's Close** (viewed by appointment, tel: 0131-529 4318), a street deserted and sealed off following a 17th-century outbreak of the plague.

At No. 180, High Street is the **Fringe Society** where tickets for the annual Festival Fringe shows can be purchased. At the junction with North Bridge is the **Tron Church**, built by John Mylne in 1647. Unused for worship since 1952, it is now an information and exhibition centre. For generations, Hogmanay revellers have gathered on the steps of the Tron Kirk on New Year's Eve.

The Tron Church

Cross over North Bridge, and the High Street broadens and continues its downward slope towards Holyrood. The medieval-style building to the right is the **Holiday Crown Plaza**, built in 1989 by Ian Begg to blend in with the surrounding vernacular architecture. Lower down the street, on the same side, is the ★★ **Museum of Childhood** ⓬ (Monday to Saturday 10am–5pm; Sundays during Edinburgh Festival, 2–5pm). It was the world's first museum on this theme and has a significant collection of historical toys, dolls and books.

★★ **Tweedale Court** ⓭ was once the home of the 1st Marquis of Tweedale, Chancellor of Scotland in 1692. The restored courtyard buildings house the **Scottish Poetry Library** and the **Saltire Society**, a group which seeks to promote and preserve Scottish culture in its widest sense.

Brass Rubbing Centre

Opposite is ★ **The Brass Rubbing Centre** (Monday to Saturday, 10am–5pm; Sundays during Edinburgh Festival, noon–5pm) in Chalmers Close. The centre occupies Trinity Apse, the remnant of what was the finest collegiate church in Scotland (founded 1460). There is a fascinating collection of replicas moulded from ancient Pictish stones, rare Scottish brasses and medieval church brasses. **Moubray House** here, restored by the Cockburn Society in 1910, is the oldest occupied dwelling in Edinburgh, said to have survived the burning of the city in 1544 by the Earl of Hertford. Daniel Defoe, author of *Robinson Crusoe*, edited the *Edinburgh Courant* from here in 1710.

Next door, on the corner, is **John Knox House** ⑭ (Monday to Saturday, 10am–5pm). This is a memorial to the religious reformer, and although it is doubtful he ever actually lived here, there is some evidence to suggest he preached from the bow-window. More accurately, it was the home of James Mossman, goldsmith to Mary Queen of Scots. There is display of relics associated with the reformer and the museum shop premises serve as the **Old Town Enquiry Centre** (tel: 0131-556 2647).

Immediately next door is the **Netherbow Arts Centre**, a small theatre, gallery space, and café. This stands on the site of Netherbow Port, the original east gate to the city, demolished in 1764.

At the junction with Jeffrey Street and St Mary's Street, you cross into the Canongate, which was once a separate burgh. At No. 83, ★ **Canongate Tolbooth** ⑮, built in 1591, was a courthouse, prison and centre of municipal affairs. A museum features ★★ **The People's Story** (Monday to Saturday 10am–5pm; Sundays during Edinburgh Festival, 2–5pm) which, with sounds, sights and smells, tells of citizens' lives over the past 200 years.

On the right hand side of the Canongate is ★★ **Huntly House** (Monday to Saturday 10am–5pm; Sundays during Edinburgh Festival, 2–5pm), a fine example of a restored 16th-century mansion which takes its name from having possibly once been the 'lodging' of the 1st Marquess of Huntly. It houses the city's principal museum of local history, containing important collections of glass, Scottish pottery and relics relating to Field Marshall Earl Haig, the World War I general. Just below Huntly House is **Acheson House**, set back from the road. Dating from the early 17th century, it was built for a Secretary of State for Scotland and restored by the 3rd Marquis of Bute in 1937.

★★ **Canongate Kirk** ⑯, on the north side, was built to replace the Abbey Church of Holyrood in 1691. In its graveyard lie Adam Smith, who wrote *The Wealth of Nations*, Horatius Bonar, the hymn writer, and the young poet Robert Fergusson, who was so much admired by Robert Burns that he erected a stone over his unmarked grave. A small plaque commemorates Scotland's three great poets, the three Roberts – Fergusson, Burns and Stevenson.

Opposite is **Queensberry House**. Originally a mansion for the 2nd Duke of Lauderdale, it was sold to the 1st Duke of Queensberry in 1686. Here in 1707 Lord Drumlanrig, Queensberry's heir, a retarded youth, spitted, roasted and

John Knox House

Woodwork, John Knox House

Canongate Tolbooth

Queen Mary's Bath-house

partially ate a servant boy from the Canongate. The building was remodelled in 1803 and in 1853 was used to house the destitute. It is currently a home for the elderly. On the left, set back from the street, is **Whitehorse Close**, an attractive courtyard of buildings dating from the 17th century. In the 18th century this was where stagecoaches to London would depart from the White Horse Inn.

At the foot of the Canongate stands **Queen Mary's Bath-house**, a quaintly shaped 16th-century building. Although it carries this name, there's no historical evidence to suggest that the Queen ever made use of it. Beside it, however, are the gates of the Palace of Holyroodhouse and Abbey Strand, comprising two 16th-century houses.

These old buildings are about to be overlooked by a new **Scottish Parliament** building, currently under construction on the left-hand side facing the palace. Directly opposite the parliament site, across Holyrood Road in a spectacular setting beneath the Salisbury Crags, is a new visitor attraction, ★★ **Dynamic Earth** ⓱ (April to October, daily 10am–6pm; November to March, Wednesday to Sunday 10am–5pm), incorporating a series of themed galleries with interactive displays on the formation and evolution of the planet.

The Queen's Ante-Chamber in the Palace of Holyroodhouse

The ★★★ **Palace of Holyroodhouse** ⓲ is among the most ancient of the residences still occupied by the British royal family. Founded in 1128 by King David I as an abbey for Augustinian canons, it takes its name from a relic believed to have been a segment from Christ's cross (*rood* means cross) which belonged to David's mother, St Margaret. James II was born here in 1430.

When James IV was betrothed to Margaret Tudor, sister of King Henry VIII of England, a royal residence of suitable proportions was assembled. Between 1529 and

1532, James V built the tower-like northwestern corner. A range to the west completed the palace when Mary, his daughter, took up residence with her second husband, Lord Darnley. Holyrood is closely associated with Mary Queen of Scots: her secretary, David Rizzio, was brutally murdered here in 1566, and Darnley died when a bomb exploded in the nearby residence of Kirk O'Field.

None of this deterred Mary's son, James VI, from making full use of the building until he departed to London in 1603. Thereafter he only returned for one brief visit, saying from London: 'This I may say of Scotland, and may truly vaunt it; here I sit and govern it with my pen. I write and it is done, and by a Clerk of the Council I govern Scotland now, which others could not do by the sword'.

David Rizzio

It was his grandson, Charles II, crowned King of Scots at Scone in 1651, who truly established this as Scotland's royal residence. He commissioned Jacob de Witt to create portraits of the 111 Scots monarchs to date for the Long Gallery; all of these are based on Charles himself.

For a time, the future James VII (James II of England), Charles's brother, took up residence in the palace, but his children, Queen Mary and Queen Anne, and the incoming Hanovarian kings lacked interest in Scotland.

In 1745, their cousin, Prince Charles Edward Stuart, in an attempt to win back the British throne for his father, the *de jure* James VIII (James III of England), occupied Holyrood for a short time before the Battle of Prestonpans, which he won. Bonnie Prince Charlie then marched his army south into England, only to turn back at Derby and be roundly defeated at Culloden in 1746.

Morning Drawing Room

George IV dropped by in 1822, although he chose to sleep elsewhere. Even Queen Victoria regarded Holyrood as a stopping-off place on the way north to her beloved Balmoral. Today, however, the Queen makes regular use of the palace, and holds an annual garden party for her Scottish subjects.

Arthur's Seat

Circling to the north and east of the palace is the 640-acre (260-hectare) Holyrood Park. Here a road encompasses the slopes of the height known as **Arthur's Seat**. Above St Margaret's Loch stand the ruins of **St Anthony's Chapel**, a medieval monastery. A footpath leads over towards the ascent to Arthur's Seat and **Salisbury Crags**, a steep ridge, where a path below the upper cliffs is known as the **Radical Road** because impoverished radical weavers under the direction of Sir Walter Scott built it in the 1820s. Arthur's Seat most probably takes its name from an Arthur who was a prince of Strathclyde in the Dark Ages, and Salisbury, from the English commander who rested his troops here in the early 14th century. East of the road is the 15th-century **St Margaret's Well**.

Route 3

Greyfriars – The Museum of Scotland and Royal Museum– The University of Edinburgh – Edinburgh Festival Theatre *(see map on pages 18–19)*

This route begins at the statue of Greyfriar's Bobby, travels east, then south, skirting the heartland of Edinburgh University towards the Edinburgh Festival Theatre.

Greyfriars churchyard

Greyfriars Bobby

The main hall of the Royal Museum

The ★ **Kirk of the Greyfriars** is situated at the top of Candlemaker Row as it runs uphill from the Grassmarket, and takes its name from the medieval Franciscan friary which stood on this spot. In 1638 the National Covenant, which took issue with the English doctrines of the Episcopalian church being forced upon the Scottish people, was signed here. Among those buried in the churchyard are George Buchanan, tutor to James VI, the Earl of Morton, Regent of Scotland from 1572 to 1578, William Adam, the architect, Allan Ramsay, the poet, Duncan Ban Macintyre, the Gaelic poet, and William Smellie, who edited the *Encyclopaedia Britannica.*

On the corner of George IV Bridge and Candlemaker Row, is the tiny statue of ★★ **Greyfriars Bobby** ⓳, the little Skye terrier who so faithfully visited his master's grave in the Greyfriars Churchyard each day for 14 years and who was immortalised by the Walt Disney studio. On his death in 1872, he was buried near to his master, just inside the entrance to the kirkyard.

Immediately to the back of the Kirk of the Greyfriars, is **George Heriot's School**, endowed by and named after the goldsmith, 'Jinglin' Geordie', who accompanied James VI to London. He became a moneylender and amassed a large fortune which he left for the care and education of orphan boys. The school was built in 1660 by William Wallace and William Ayton, and subsequently improved by John and Robert Mylne, and it is now co-educational. Immediately across Lauriston Place is the Royal Infirmary of Edinburgh, the work of John and David Bryce in the late 19th century.

Across George IV Bridge is **Chambers Street**, dating from an 1860s improvement scheme. It is named after the Lord Provost of the time, William Chambers, who founded the publishing company which still bears his name and whose statue stands in the centre of the street. On the north side, the former Heriot-Watt University building has been remodelled into the **Sheriff Courthouse**.

On the south side, at the corner of Chambers Street and George IV Bridge, stands the imposing sandstone-clad ★★★ **Museum of Scotland** ⓴ (Monday to Saturday 10am–5pm, Tuesday to 8pm; Sunday noon–5pm), com-

The Royal Museum

pleted in 1998 to bring under one roof some of Scotland's most valuable national treasures and tell the country's history. Next door is the magnificent 19th-century ★★★ **Royal Museum** (Monday to Saturday 10am–5pm, Tuesday to 8pm; Sunday noon–5pm). Designed by Francis Fowke, it was built between 1861 and 1885. The 270-ft (82-metre) main hall, which is roofed in glass, is often used for receptions and banquets. The Royal Museum is the largest museum in the UK outside London and it has a superb collections of natural history, 30,000 fossil fishes, scientific implements, and examples of Asiatic sculpture and Chinese and Islamic decorative art.

The Golden Boy

At the east end, Chambers Street meets South Bridge, behind which, to the southeast, is the University of Edinburgh's **Old College** ㉑, where the dome is surmounted by the small statue of **The Golden Boy**, carrying the torch of knowledge. Robert Adam's design was completed in 1834 by William Playfair, who was responsible for the interior designs. The **Talbot Rice Art Gallery** (Tuesday to Saturday 10am–5pm; during Edinburgh Festival, Monday to Saturday 10am–5pm, Sunday 2–5pm) in the college is a popular venue for contemporary art exhibitions.

The University buildings of George Square and the McEwan Hall, which accommodates the Student Union, range behind. George Square was begun in the late 18th century by James Brown, who named it after his brother. It was largely bulldozed by the university in the central redevelopment plan of the 1960s, but the west side and part of the east side remain intact.

The Festival Theatre

Further along from South Bridge where the road becomes Nicolson Street, is the glass-fronted ★★★ **Edinburgh Festival Theatre** ㉒, converted from the old Empire Theatre in 1994 by architects Law & Dunbar-Nasmith. Several theatres have occupied this site, notably the one which caught fire in 1811 causing the death on stage of the Great Lafayette, the celebrated illusionist from America. The present structure has 2,000 seats and an extended stage area larger than that of the Royal Opera House, Convent Garden.

Opposite stands the ★ **Royal College of Surgeons of Edinburgh** ㉓, again the work of William Playfair. The ★ **Playfair Museum of Pathology and Anatomy** (viewing by appointment, tel: 0131-527 1649) houses a collection of rather disturbing anatomical items kept in jars. Adjacent is the **Menzies Campbell Dental Museum** (Monday to Friday 2–4pm) and at No. 9, Hill Square, the **Sir Jules Thorn Exhibition of the History of Surgery** (Monday to Friday, 2–4pm).

At play on the Meadows

On the right hand side, along Clerk Street, is the **Queen's Hall**, a Georgian church designed by Robert Brown in 1823. It hosts a wide range of concerts and entertainments throughout the year (enquiries, tel: 0131-668 3456). At the end of Clerk Street, the road to the right leads to the **Meadows**, a Burgh Loch before the 18th century, but now a green open space providing a range of recreational facilities. Opened as a public park in 1860, the Meadows were reclaimed a hundred of so years previously by Thomas Hope of Rankeillour, the president of the Society of Improvers of the Knowledge of Agriculture in Scotland.

The road to the east connects with Dalkeith Road, where the Scottish Widows Fund & Life Assurance Society occupies a striking, hexagonal building faced in dark glass. A short distance from here is the ★ **Royal Commonwealth Pool** ㉔ (tel: 0131-667 7211 for opening times), built for the Commonwealth Games of 1970, has swimming, sauna and weight-training facilities in addition to flumes. Next door are the University of Edinburgh's Pollock Halls of Residence, which back onto Holyrood Park.

Duddingston Loch, where the the Rev. Robert Walker skated in Raeburn's painting

To the northeast, approached through the park, is the well-preserved **Duddingston Village**, named for a 12th-century Norman knight of the name of Dodin, who leased the land from the Abbot of Kelso. **Duddingston Kirk** dates from the 12th century, with later additions, and **Duddingston Loch** – where Sir Henry Raeburn set his famous portrait of the Rev. Robert Walker skating – is now a bird sanctuary. In the early 19th century, the Rev. John Thomson, minister of the kirk, was an accomplished artist, having studied under Alexander Nasmyth, the landscape painter and pupil of Allan Ramsay, Jr. Thomson's Tower, his studio on the lochside, he called 'Edinburgh', so that when visitors came to call, his servants could honestly say that their master was in Edinburgh. The **Sheep's Heid Inn** dates from the 16th century when James VI is said to have presented the owner with a silver ram's head.

St James Square – Calton Hill – Waterloo Place – Princes Street – The Mound *(see map on pages 18–19)*

This route begins in front of St Mary's Cathedral at the east end of the New Town, and scales Calton Hill.

St Mary's Catholic Cathedral ㉕ designed by James Gillespie Graham in 1813, was the first Roman Catholic church to be built in Edinburgh after the Reformation. A fire in 1878 left only the facade. On the terracing in front of the cathedral, facing Picardy Place, are three statues which include a giant foot and a hand by the sculptor Sir Eduardo Paolozzi, born in 1924 in nearby Leith. These symbolise the strong connections between Edinburgh and the Italian families from Bargos and Monte Cassino who came to the city at the end of the 19th century.

Located on Picardy Place, on the north side of the square, is a statue of Sherlock Holmes by Gerald Ogilvy Laing. This commemorates the birth in 1859 of Holmes's creator, Sir Arthur Conan Doyle, whose family occupied a now demolished tenement flat in the centre of the square.

★★★ **Calton Hill**, another volcanic outcrop, sits at the east end of the New Town. It is approached either by a short walk down Greenside Place, past the ★ **Playhouse Theatre** ㉖, originally Edinburgh's largest cinema, seating 3,000, into Blenheim Place where a pathway leads onto steps. Or you can go up Leith Street and take the steep, cobbled road called Calton Hill which branches off to the left and connects with Waterloo Place at the top.

From the summit of Calton Hill there are panoramic views of the Old Town, the New Town, Holyrood Palace and Arthur's Seat, the Firth of Forth, and beyond to the

Paolozzi's hand

The view from Calton Hill

The Nelson Monument

open sea. In summer this is a favourite dropping-off point for tourist coaches. Much of the building dotted around the top of the hill and below dates from just after the end of the Napoleonic Wars in which Scottish soldiers played a significant role.

The **City Observatory** ㉗ has a Grecian-style dome and was designed by Sir William Playfair in 1818. Beneath the octagonal **City Dome** is the ★★★ **Edinburgh Experience**, an audio-visual, three-dimensional celebration of the city. (Performances half-hourly April to October, daily 10.30am–5pm.)

On the north side of the hill is the ★★★ **Nelson Monument** ㉘ (April to September, Monday 1–6pm, Tuesday to Saturday 10am–6pm; October to March, 10am–3pm) erected in 1807 to celebrate the Trafalgar naval victory. It's worth climbing the spiral stair to the lookout platform on a clear day. The 1 o'clock Time Ball is dropped to coincide with the gun fired from Edinburgh Castle.

With its sights trained on the length of Princes Street, a cannon squats defensively nearby, and to the west, the imposing ★ **Dugald Stewart's Monument** commemorates a distinguished professor of philosophy at Edinburgh University. Crowning the summit is **Rock House**, 19th-century home of the pioneering photographer David Octavius Hill. On the centre portion of the hill, the 12 pillars of the ★★ **National Monument** ㉙ honour the soldiers killed in the Napoleonic Wars. It was intended that this should be a full-scale replica of the Parthenon in Athens, but only the west side was completed before funds ran out.

Immediately below Calton Hill on Waterloo Place is the **Old Royal High School**, a Greek Doric building designed by Thomas Hamilton in 1829 and altered during the 1970s to serve as the proposed **Scottish Assembly**. On the far side of Regent Road is the 1830 Greek-temple style ★ **Burns Monument**, again designed by Thomas Hamilton. It overlooks the **New Calton Burial Ground**, which dates from 1821. Across the street from here, Regent Terrace curls around the northern slopes of Calton Hill to meet Royal Terrace, both named to commemorate George IV's visit to the city in 1822. Royal Terrace was designed by Playfair, and its three sets of seven, 10 and another seven giant Corinthian colonnades have balustrades between them all with arched entrances and ground-floor windows.

Towards the east end of Princes Street, on the left hand side, is **St Andrews House**, Thomas Tait's 1939 Scottish Office headquarters, built on the site of the Calton Jail, once Scotland's largest prison. Of this, only the mock medieval tower known as the **Governor's House** survives.

In the section that remains of the ★ **Old Calton Burial Ground** ㉚ lie many of the great names of Scotland's enlightenment period, including David Hume, the philoso-

The National Monument

The Burns Monument

pher. The obelisk, erected in 1844, commemorates Thomas Muir, the exiled revolutionary, and other 18th-century political martyrs. George E. Bissell's 1893 ★ **Emancipation Monument**, depicting Abraham Lincoln with a slave kneeling at his feet, is in memory of Scottish soldiers who died fighting in the American Civil War.

Register House, with Wellington's statue

At the east end of Princes Street, as Regent Road meets Waterloo Place, stands the former General Post Office building. The work of Robert Matheson, it was built on the site of the former Theatre Royal. Opposite is ★ **Register House**, designed by Robert and James Adam, and in 1774 the first major work to be started in the New Town. It is one of the first buildings to have been built for the purpose of storing public records and it incorporates 100 vaulted rooms within thick stone walls to combat fire risk. The statue on the pavement in front depicts the 1st Duke of Wellington on horseback.

Immediately next door, set back from the roadway, is the **Court of the Lord Lyon King of Arms**, headquarters of Scotland's ultimate heraldic and genealogical authority. Facing it, on the opposite corner of North Bridge, is the **Balmoral Hotel**, built by Sir William Hamilton Beattie in 1902 for the North British Railway Company.

Princes Street piper

Until 1799, Princes Street was largely residential. By 1846, however, a railway line had opened. Residents asked Sir William Playfair, whose hand is seen in almost every corner of the east end of Edinburgh, to mask the intruder with a wall and embankment. Today this space is the site of the multi-level ★★ **Waverley Shopping Centre** ㉛ which incorporates a Tourist Information Office.

Across Waverley Bridge, a statue of David Livingstone, the missionary and explorer, is set back in the gardens. Beyond is the figure of Adam Black, twice Lord Provost of Edinburgh, and one-time member of parliament. Nearby is a statue of Professor John Wilson, who wrote many popular articles under the pen-name of Christopher North.

Statue of Scott under the Scott Monument, and the Balmoral Hotel

The erection of the 180-ft (55-metre) **Scott Monument** ㉜ (currently being restored; reopening late 2000 or 2001 with a new historical exhibition) began in 1840, eight years after the death of the novelist Sir Walter Scott, Edinburgh's most famous citizen. Its mix of Gothic fantasy and pure romanticism was the work of George Meikle Kemp, winner of an open architectural competition. Sadly, Kemp was never to see his creation completed: he drowned in the Union Canal while the construction work was underway.

Within the monument is a statue of Sir Walter with Maida, his favourite staghound. The exterior stone incorporates more than 60 statuettes of characters from his books. The 287 steps can be climbed when public access is returned.

Route 5

The Mound – Princes Street – Shandwick Place – Charlotte Square – St Andrew Square *(see map on pages 18–19)*

This route begins half-way along Princes Street on the steps of Royal Scottish Academy, and explores the handsome Georgian New Town.

Royal Scottish Academy

The Mound was originally built as a link path between old and new Edinburgh, constructed of rubble dug out of the foundations of the New Town. By an Act of Parliament in 1816, the town council was authorised to build on it according to a plan agreed in consultation with a group of Princes Street residents, with a subsequent guarantee that gardens should be preserved as an open space, but it wasn't until 1830 that a proper road was constructed.

At the foot of the Mound stands the ★★★ **Royal Scottish Academy** ㉝ (tel: 0131-225 6671 or 0131-225 5945 for exhibition opening times), erected in 1826 and surmounted by a statue of Queen Victoria by Sir John Steell. Behind this magnificent building is the no less splendid ★★★ **National Gallery of Scotland** ㉞ (Monday to Saturday 10am–6pm, Sunday 2–6pm), which houses one of the best art collections in Europe. The Scottish collection is outstanding, and there are fine examples of the majority of the old masters. Turner watercolours are displayed annually in January. Both galleries were designed by William Playfair in addition to the adjacent flight of steps which lead to the top of the Mound. In 1978, through the insistence of the Cockburn Society, their name was changed from John Knox Way to the **Playfair Steps**.

The National Gallery of Scotland

At the foot of the Mound, on the other side of the road,

is the world's oldest ★ **Floral Clock** ㉟, laid out annually with more than 20,000 plants; it has electrically driven hands. **Princes Street Gardens**, below the castle rock, was once the Nor' Loch which served as the city's defensive moat against the approach from the north. Draining began in 1759 with the object of creating pleasure gardens for the exclusive use of New Town residents, but today they are open to all.

The Floral Clock

Princes Street, named after the sons of George III, contains, along the south side, various statues inserted into the gardens. Allan Ramsay, the poet, again by Steell, is first. Then there is Sir Frank Mears's memorial to the Royal Scots, the Edinburgh regiment which is the oldest of the line of the British army and served, according to the legend, with Pontius Pilate's Bodyguard in Scotland. Further along is Birnie Rhynd's equestrian statue paying tribute to yet another famous Scottish regiment, the Royal Scots Greys. The most recent memorial to be placed in these gardens is the work of Ian Hamilton Finlay, the concrete poet; it commemorates Robert Louis Stevenson who, exiled for health reasons in the South Seas, yearned to return to the 'precipitous city' of his childhood.

The **Ross Bandstand**, which has seating for spectators, has now become a popular seasonal venue for concerts and dancing. It is used for the annual Edinburgh Festival Firework Concert.

St John's Episcopal Church (left) and St Cuthbert's Kirk

At the West End of Princes Street, **Lothian Road** turns south at a right angle on the corner with **St John's Episcopal Church** ㊱, leading to Edinburgh's recently relocated and purpose-built financial and international conference centres. St John's Church, designed by William Burn in 1818, was partly modelled on St George's Chapel at Windsor Castle. The interior celebrates the Gothic revival in Scotland and the stained-glass windows are truly spectacular.

Tucked away behind St John's, as Kings Stable Road curls round the castle, **St Cuthbert's Kirk** is located in the gardens. The present church, said to occupy the site of an 8th-century monastery, was built in 1894 and, during the excavation work, the foundations of six earlier churches were discovered. Within the present church there are murals by John Duncan, and a fresco of St Cuthbert on Lindisfarne by Gerald Moira. In the kirkyard are the graves of Alexander Nasmyth, George Meikle Kemp, the ill-fated designer of the Scott Monument, and Thomas de Quincey, author of *Confessions of an Opium Eater*.

Straight ahead of Princes Street, with the **Caledonian Hotel** (with liveried doormen) on the corner of Rutland Street, is Shandwick Place, which leads west towards Haymarket. At the end of Shandwick place are Atholl Crescent and Coates Crescent, which features a statue of

Strolling in Charlotte Square

The Georgian House

George Street

William Ewart Gladstone (1809–98) several times Britain's prime minister.

The elegant New Town of Edinburgh is built on a grid system of broad streets, running in parallels. Charlotte Square on the west is linked by George Street, behind Princes Street, to St Andrew Square to the east. **Charlotte Square**, with a central garden featuring the equestrian **Albert Memorial** statue by Sir John Steell, is considered the finest square in the city, and is dominated by the domed St George's Church, today known as ★ **West Register House**, and occupied by the Scottish Record Office. Designed by Robert Adam in 1791, the square is named after Queen Charlotte, the wife of George III, who had 15 children and died in 1818.

Once entirely residential, the square is now mainly occupied by commercial concerns. The north side is considered Adam's greatest neo-classical urban masterpiece, with No. 5, the headquarters of the National Trust for Scotland, and No. 6, known as **Bute House**, the official residence of the Secretary of State for Scotland.

Previously owned by the family of the Marquess of Bute, the three floors of No. 7, the ★★★ **Georgian House** ㊲ (1 April to 31 October, Monday to Saturday 10am–5pm; Sunday 2–5pm; parties of 20 or more should book in advance; entry fee is expensive) have been refurbished by the National Trust for Scotland in the style of 1796. There is a fascinating array of china, silver, pictures and furniture, gadgets and utensils ranging from the decorative to the purely functional. Adjacent to the museum shop is an audio-visual room which describes the life of Edinburgh's New Town.

The Georgian character of **George Street**, named after George III, remains relatively unspoiled, with a number of quality shops. Statues, at intersections, honour famous men: Dr Thomas Chalmers, first principal of Free Church College, at Castle Street; William Pitt, the British prime minister, at Frederick Street, and George IV at Hanover Street.

On the north side, between Frederick Street and Hanover Street, are the **Assembly Rooms** ㊳, originated by James Henderson in 1818, but later added to by William Burn, who with William Bryce added the **Music Hall** at the rear. With their magnificent crystal chandeliers, the Assembly Rooms have been the venue for many a great social occasion, and are now used as a Festival Fringe and occasional ceilidh venue. Between Hanover Street and St Andrew Square, across from the George Hotel, the **Royal College of Physicians** (access by arrangement) dates from 1844. It was designed by Thomas Hamilton with additions by David Bryce.

St Andrew Square, much altered by modern buildings in the latter half of the 20th century, retains a few of its original facades. The gardens at its centre are dominated by the 121-ft (37-metre) ★ **Melville Monument**, a Doric column surmounted by a statue by Robert Forrest of Henry Dundas, 1st Viscount Melville, who as a key figure in Pitt the Younger's government influenced Scottish politics to the extent that he became known as 'The Uncrowned King of Scotland'.

Melville Monument

On the east side of the square, set back from the roadway is the ★★ **Royal Bank of Scotland** ㊴, once the home of Melville's kinsman, Sir Laurence Dundas, a wealthy member of parliament who reputedly gambled away his home in a game of poker. Later an Excise Office, the mansion was purchased by the bank in 1825 and refurbished with a magnificent domed banking hall which features on all their bank notes. The equestrian statue to the front, by Thomas Campbell in 1834, depicts the 4th Earl of Hopetoun, a hero of the Napoleonic Wars and a governor of the bank.

From the parallel routes of Princes Street, George Street and Queen Street, the New Town drops downhill towards Stockbridge, Comely Bank and Inverleith, encompassing the pattern of squares, closes and crescents devised in James Craig's award-winning 18th-century plan. As seemed appropriate for a major Georgian city of the United Kingdom, north sloping streets were named after the reigning Hanovarian monarchy: Frederick Street, after George III's father, and Hanover Street, commemorating the six Hanovarian monarchs prior to the reign of Queen Victoria. North and South St David Street commemorate the patron saint of Wales, and St Andrew Square is named after the patron saint of Scotland, crucified on a diagonal cross which was to inspire the white cross on a blue background of the Scottish Saltire flag.

The Royal Bank of Scotland

Queen Street, which runs parallel to George Street, was again named after George III's wife, Queen Charlotte. At the east end is the ★★★ **Scottish National Portrait Gallery** ㊵ (Monday to Saturday, 10am–5pm, Sunday 2–5pm). Housed in red-sandstone Gothic splendour, the museum contains fine portraits of celebrated Scots including Robert Burns by Alexander Nasmyth, Robert Louis Stevenson by Count Nerlie, Mary Queen of Scots by Oeter Oudry, and more contemporary portraits such as Sir Steven Runciman, the historian, by Stephen Conroy. Designed by R. Rowand Anderson in 1890, the building was a gift to the Scottish nation from J. R. Finlay who owned *The Scotsman* newspaper. The magnificent restored murals which surround the ceiling of the front hall are by the early 20th-century artist Phoebe Traquair. On the exterior is historical statuary by W. Birnie Rhynd.

Facade of the Portrait Gallery

The Royal Circus

An elegant address

Moray Place

Below Queen Street, to the northwest, are the town houses of **Northumberland Street** and **Great King Street** leading into **Drummond Place**, **Cumberland Street** and **Fettes Row**, largely designed by Robert Reid in 1802. In 1822, William Playfair added the two-winged **Royal Circus**. Originally, the substantial buildings of these sweeping architectural masterpieces were designed for Edinburgh's professional classes, with servants' quarters sometimes located at the end of streets and stable accommodation behind. Except for a few hotel developments and some offices, nearly all the townhouses are now divided into flats.

All the streets off Queen Street reflect the period of their creation. **Abercrombie Place**, designed by Robert Reid in 1805, overlooks **Queen Street Gardens** and is named after Sir Ralph Abercrombie (1734–1801), hero of the Seven Years' War, a major European conflict which lasted from 1756 to 1763. **Dundas Street** (now home to half a dozen private art galleries), which evolved from 1807, was named for Henry Dundas, 1st Viscount Melville (1742–1811), whose statue stands in St Andrew Square, and **Howe Street**, leading downhill towards Royal Circus, is named for Richard, 1st Earl Howe (1726–99), a celebrated admiral of the Seven Years' War.

Heriot Row was built by Robert Reid in 1802, but in 1864 additions were added by David Bryce. It is named after George Heriot, who bankrolled James VI on his journey to London, and in 1857, No. 17 became the home of Thomas Stevenson, father of Robert Louis Stevenson, whose childhood memories here inspired *Treasure Island* (1881) and his poem, *Leerie the Lamplighter*. (The novelist also commentated on the decay into which some of the New Town was allowed to fall in the late 19th century: 'It is as much a matter of course to decry the New Town as to exalt the Old; and the most celebrated authorities have picked out this quarter as the very emblem of what is condemned in architecture.')

Edinburgh town planners have introduced some rather inexplicable 'traffic-calming' measures and, to the bewilderment of many of the residents, **Moray Place** now has car access only from **Gloucester Place**, named for Frederick, 2nd Duke of Gloucester (1776–1834) and **Darnaway Street**, called after the Earl of Moray's Morayshire estate. This does, however, make for a quieter city-centre existence, although Moray Place, linked for pedestrians to **St Colme Street** by **Forrest Street**, and to Ainslie Place above by **Great Stuart Street**, is always filled to capacity with parked cars.

Moray Place, considered one of Edinburgh's most prestigious residential addresses, was built on land once owned by Mary Queen of Scots' illegitimate brother, the Earl of Moray (1531–70). It has a 12-sided design by James Gillespie Graham. Aisnlie Place is named after the 10th Earl of Moray's second wife, Margaret Ainslie of Pilton.

From above Ainslie Place, **Randolph Crescent** horseshoes into Queensferry Street. Built in the 1820s, it comprises appealing arched doorways with Roman Doric pilasters, and is named after Sir Thomas Randolph (d. 1332), Robert the Bruce's nephew.

Queensferry Street initiates the first stage of the main road towards the former ferry, now bridge, crossing of the Firth of Forth. On the far side, the New Town extends down **Melville Street** and **Melville Crescent**, both designed by Robert Brown in 1814. At the centre of the crescent is a statue of Robert Dundas, 2nd Viscount Melville (1771–1851), by John Steell. The majority of the buildings in this area are commercial offices, although as you progress west to **Palmerston Place**, named after the 3rd Viscount Palmerston (1784–1865), the British Prime Minister, the houses become almost exclusively residential.

Fronting onto Palmerston Place and backing onto **Manor Place** is **St Mary's Episcopal Cathedral** ㊶, considered the finest church to be built in Scotland since the Reformation. Designed by Sir George Gilbert Scott in 1879, it was funded by a legacy from Barbara and Mary Walker, two spinster ladies, the heiresses of Sir Patrick Walker (1777–1837), a wealthy advocate and landowner, who resided at nearby Easter Coates. Their original, small mansion house to the side of the cathedral houses the **St Mary's Music School**, which is internationally known.

Between here and Haymarket, which before the inner city ring road was opened was Edinburgh's main exit road towards Glasgow and Stirling, the crescents of Grosvenor, Glencairn, Eglinton, Douglas and Magdala mainly comprise private residences and flats.

Viscount Melville

St Mary's Episcopal Cathedral and its Music School choir

Route 6

Stockbridge – St Bernard's Well – The Dean Village – The Scottish National Gallery of Modern Art *(see map on pages 18–19)*

Stockbridge blooms

Ann Street, Stockbridge

Popular with strollers

This is a pleasant stroll along beside the **Water of Leith**, starting at Stockbridge and going upriver towards the Dean Village. Edinburgh's river is an attractive ribbon of silver and green which flows from the Firth of Forth at Leith, snaking through the city to the west and beyond into the Pentland Hills. In recent years the riverside walkway has been lovingly restored by the Water of Leith Walkway Trust, using funds from the municipal Job Creation Scheme. As a result, natural wildlife, fish and flora have returned to what, for many years, had been a muddy, overgrown trickle of water.

Stockbridge, named after the original footbridge spanning the river and used by livestock, is a bustling shopping and residential centre to the northwest of the New Town. This district grew largely under the influence of Henry Raeburn, the great Scottish portrait painter. As part of a commercial housing development, from 1813 onwards, as a birthday present for his wife, he built the elegant ★★ **Ann Street**, once described by the English poet Sir John Betjeman as 'the most attractive street in Britain'.

Stockbridge was further enlarged by an 1860s housing development known as the ★ **Stockbridge Colonies** ㊷, 11 rows of terraced houses designed for artisans serving the New Town. A particular feature of the gable ends of each block is the stone carvings of tools and implements belonging to different trades.

Extending east is Henderson Row which fronts on to **Edinburgh Academy**, erected in 1824 by private subscription to a design by William Burn to provide education for the sons of the New Town (daughters were regarded as being less worthy of serious education). **St Stephen's Church**, which sprawls at the foot of Frederick Street in the New Town, was built by William Playfair in 1827 and there is an unlikely tale that the bulk was intentional in order to hide the view of the pristine, neoclassical Edinburgh Academy from Princes Street. Parallel with Henderson Row, adjoining North West Circus Place, is St Stephen's Street, which is filled with interesting curio and bric-a-brac shops. Stockbridge has become a characterful district within easy walking distance of Princes Street. The present stone bridge was built in 1902, replacing a former bridge from 1786.

From Deanhaugh Terrace, and the corner of Stockbridge, steps lead off onto the ★★★ **Water of Leith**

Walkway and the Deanhaugh Footpath, opened in 1981. Another access point to the Walkway is at the end of India Place. ★★ **St Bernard's Well** 43 (viewing inside by arrangement with Edinburgh District Council), situated on the riverbank, is a small, circular Roman temple, complete with a statue of Hygeia, the Greek goddess of health. The tradition is that the spring was discovered by three schoolboys fishing in the river in 1760, and thereafter became popular for the supposed healing powers of its mineral spring. A plaque acknowledges the purchase and restoration of the well by Willimina Nelson, who bequeathed it to the city in 1888.

St Bernard's Well

The pathway continues thereafter under the towering, four-arch ★★ **Dean Bridge** 44, built by Thomas Telford in 1832, and rising 106ft (32 metres) above the river. For many years, until the parapets were raised in 1912, this was renowned as a favourite suicide spot.

The ★ **Zyw Gallery** 45, up on Bell's Brae, commemorates the painter Aleksander Zyw, who imported olive oil and had a studio here. **Well Court** is a surprising square of red Teutonic-style residential buildings, a Victorian experiment in community dwelling by the philanthropist J.R. Findlay, proprietor of the Scotsman newspaper. The clock tower, now an architect's office, was once the community hall.

Well Court

A swift flow at Damhead Weir

From Bell's Brae, a steep, narrow road leads from Queensferry Street and the Dean Bridge above to the ★★ **Dean Village** 46, taken from *dene* or *dean*, meaning 'deep valley'. Prior to the building of the Dean Bridge, travellers towards Queensferry would have to descend Bell's Brae and cross the old bridge to climb up the steep other side of the gorge.The Water of Leith Walk meanwhile skirts the base of the steep gorge, and passes the **Damhead Weir**, a rush of bubbling water which once powered many of the mills here. Dean Village is around a corner, sunken into the hollow out-of-sight from the high town above.

First granted to the canons of Holyrood in 1143, at one time the Baker's Guild operated 11 water mills here, manufacturing all the meal for Edinburgh and the surrounding villages. This industry went into rapid decline with larger, more modern mills opening in Leith during the 19th century. Similarly, the Dean Tannery, which once processed sheepskins, was demolished in 1973. In this picturesque hideaway, it is hard to recall that the bustle and traffic of the town is less than half a mile away. Secluded and hidden from view, there has been a considerable amount of residential, vernacular-style, building in recent years.

From the Dean Village, follow Hawthornbank Lane until you come to the footbridge over the ancient ford. Access

Belford Bridge

Donaldson's College

In the grounds of the Scottish National Gallery of Modern Art

to the **Dean Cemetery**, laid out in the grounds of the demolished Dean House in the Victorian era, is from Dean Path, and among the prominent Edinburgh citizens interred here are Lord Cockburn, W.H. Playfair, Sam Bough, the painter, David Octavius Hill, the photographer, and Dr Elsie Inglis, who founded the Scottish Women's Suffragette Movement. The cemetery is noted for having a fine collection of sculptures and architectural monuments.

The 1887 **Belford Bridge** is the start of the **Dean Bank footpath**, constructed on ground handed over to the city by the Dean Cemetery Trustees in 1975. On the left-hand side of Belford Road is the Hilton National Hotel, on a site where milling has taken place for more than 800 years. An explosion in 1971 destroyed the last of the two Bell's Mills, but the granary and miller's house survive.

Out-of-sight, high on the left bank, is **Donaldson's College**. Designed by William Playfair in 1841, it became a school for the deaf in 1938. Queen Victoria is said to have remarked in 1850 that it was finer than any of her palaces in Scotland. Also off Belford Road is the Edinburgh Sports Club, a private tennis and squash establishments, and on the far side is the ★★★ **Dean Gallery** (Monday to Saturday 10am–5pm, Sunday 2–5pm), built by Thomas Hamilton in 1833 as an Orphan Hospital. Today it is used to display the works of the Edinburgh-born artist, Sir Eduardo Paolozzi, and the National Galleries' Dada and Surrealist collections. Fabricated in Craigleith Stone, this imposing baroque-style building has a two-storey attic on top of the portico which features the clock of the old Netherbow.

In close proximity is the ★★★ **Scottish National Gallery of Modern Art** ㊼ (Monday to Saturday 10am–5pm, Sunday 2–5pm), housed in a building originally designed in 1825 by William Burn for John Watson's Hospital and School, which merged with George Watson's College in 1975. Scotland's national collection of 20th-century paintings, sculptures, and graphics was founded in 1960 and located at Inverleith House in the Royal Botanic Gardens until 1984. There are works by major British, European and American artists including Bonnard, Duthy, Giacometti, Matisse, Miró, Picasso and Vuillard. Scottish art is strongly represented with Scottish Colourists such as Peploe, Cadell and Hunter, also Robert Colquhoun, Joan Eardlie and John Bellany. The 12 acres (5 hectares) of grounds feature pieces of sculpture by Sir Henry Moore, Barbara Hepworth and Jacob Epstein. There is a souvenir shop, and a pleasant, friendly café is situated within the building.

Rejoining the Water of Leith Walkway, the path leads to **Coltbridge** and the **Coltbridge Viaduct**, which now carries a cycleway on the track of the former railway line.

Botanical browsing

Route 7

Inverleith and the Royal Botanic Garden *(see map on pages 18–19)*

This route begins at West Gate of Royal Botanic Garden just to the north west of the New Town and a mile north of the city centre. Bus services 8, 19, 23, 27 and 37 stop at the East Gate on Inverleith Row. There is ample unrestricted on-street car parking near the West Gate in Arboretum Place.

The district of Inverleith is dominated by the imposing spire and bulk of **Fettes College**, designed by David Bryce in 1870 and founded as an independent school for boys, although it now admits girl pupils. To the east is **Inverleith Park**, a popular recreational area for football, tennis, and cricket on a seasonal basis.

★★★ **The Royal Botanic Garden** (daily from 9.30am; closes at dusk in winter, at 7pm April to September), founded in 1824, is situated in 70 acres (28 hectares) of superb landscaping. Exotic, beautiful and bizarre plants are to be found in this world-famous garden which evolved from the Physic Gardens established near Holyrood Abbey in 1670, and which have been on their present site since 1820. Sir Robert Sibbald, physician to Charles II and first Professor of Medicine at Edinburgh University, and Sir Andrew Balfour had the inspiration to start the garden, being primarily interested in the medicinal properties of plants. A network of footpaths lead on a journey of exploration. Attractions include the Rock Garden, Chinese and Woodland Gardens, with some of the finest rhododendrons in the UK, the Arboretum, and the Glasshouse Experience. The orchid and palm houses are particularly spectacular.

Fettes College

The Royal Botanic Garden

Bowling at Inverleith Park

Arboretum Avenue was formerly the entrance to ★★ **Inverleith House** (48), a Georgian mansion house built for the Rocheid family, which stands at the centre of the gardens and hosts botanic-related art exhibitions. One of the best panoramic views of the city's skyline can be enjoyed from the back lawn of Inverleith House.

Beside the West Gate is the Botanic Shop and Dill's Snack Bar. The Terrace Café, next to Inverleith House, is licensed and serves a full range of meals.

To the east of the gardens is **Canonmills** where the Canons of Holyrood Abbey, granted lands by David I in the 12th century, established a water mill on the Water of Leith. Robert Louis Stevenson was born here in Howard Place in 1850 and spent much of his childhood in the Inverleith area before his parents moved to Heriot Row in the New Town. He fished on a nearby stretch of river.

The Water of Leith Walkway connects from Warriston Crescent, having crossed Inverleith Row, and a plaque at No. 10 commemorates the visit of Frederic Chopin in 1848, the year before his death. Warriston Cycleway follows the line to Leith Citadel Station, built by the North British Railway company in 1849 during the Victorian railway boom. It closed to passenger services in 1947 and the local authority, having acquired the Junction Bridge Railway Depot, renamed Coalie Park, acquired the railway line to Warriston in order to open the Walkway.

Chopin was here

On the far side of the river is **Powderhall Stadium** (49), laid out in 1869 as a state-of-the-art sports stadium. It was the location of the first Scottish Amateur Athletic Association Championship and at the final meeting in 1922, Eric Liddell, subject of the Oscar-winning 1981 film *Chariots of Fire*, won both sprint events. For many years the stadium was the home of regular greyhound racing meetings but is now closed, awaiting redevelopment.

Route 8

The Port and Town of Leith – Leith Links – The Shore – Lamb's House

Leith is the port of Edinburgh, on the Firth of Forth, and is reached down Leith Walk which runs from the east end of Princes Street. It is served by a number of buses. The earliest record of Leith being inhabited is in a reference of 1143. From the 14th until the mid-19th centuries it served as Scotland's foremost port, trading with the Low Countries, France and the Baltic. In the 16th century it was twice attacked and almost destroyed by the English.

Restaurant-ship at Leith

In 1548, the Catholic Mary of Guise, Governor of Scotland during her daughter Mary Queen of Scots' infancy, made Leith her seat of government and, when threatened by the anti-Catholic sentiments which led to the Reformation, she raised fortifications to defend the town. After her death two years later, these were pulled down by her triumphant Protestant opponents.

A century later, a plague was to kill 2,000, almost two-thirds of the population, but by the start of the 18th century, Leith had established a major reputation for the building of timber vessels, and even Peter the Great of Russia paid a visit to learn about shipbuilding and, having done so, went home to create his own fleet in the Baltic.

In 1698 the ill-fated Darien Expedition set sail from Leith. A company had been set up in 1685 to trade with Africa and the Indies, with power to establish colonies. A combination of the climate, tropical disease and the hostility of the Spaniards, who had their own colonial aspirations, coupled with the refusal of Westminster to give assistance, led to the financial ruin of many Scottish families who had invested heavily in the project.

In 1720, Britain's first dry dock was built in Leith, and in 1779 Paul Jones, the Scottish-born American renegade, made an abortive attempt to capture the port with a small French squadron displaying American

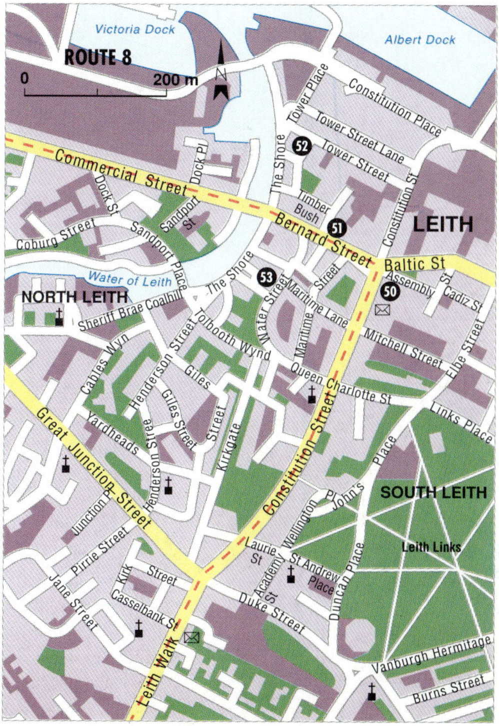

colours. Although activity boomed during the Napoleonic Wars, shipbuilding began to change in the 19th century with the introduction of iron hulls. Lacking the necessary deep-water facilities, Leith could not compete with rival ports and went rapidly into decline.

Incorporation with Edinburgh didn't come about until 1920, but the port and town still retained a fierce individuality. Indeed, many old Leithers still do not consider themselves to be citizens of Edinburgh. Despite this feeling for tradition, the massive programme of renovations which has taken place since the early 1980s has drastically altered the character of the place. The promotional slogan 'Leith-sur-Mer' has encouraged fashionable restaurants and up-market housing amid the fine merchant buildings of a prosperous past. To engender a sense of the new, there are large, colourful, out-of-doors murals painted on the side of some of the buildings, such as on Bonnington Road and on the corner of North Junction Street. Recent newcomers to the area are the purpose-built headquarters of the Scottish Office and, in the docks, the decommissioned **Royal Yacht Britannia** (visitor centre and yacht open daily 10.30am–4.30pm).

Kirkgate Shopping Centre

At the same time, links with the European continent remain strong, having their origins in the wine trade. This was such a major business that, during the Napoleonic Wars, Edinburgh's City Council voted to ban the import of French claret, in order to 'bring France to its knees.' Today, Leith claret and French wines are as popular as ever, and as Leith emerges into a new era of prosperity, it has been assisted by funding from the European Union.

Tree planting and wrought-iron work on the fine, wide Leith Walk give the approach to the port a suitably prosperous air. At the foot of Leith Walk, close to the entrance of the **Kirkgate Shopping Centre**, stands a statue of Queen Victoria, who arrived in her yacht, the *Royal George*, in 1842, but put ashore at Granton, along the coast. To the right, Duke Street leads to ★★ **Leith Links** where the Honourable Company of Edinburgh Golfers established their first clubhouse in the late 18th century. Today this august body is established at Muirfield on the East Lothian coast, but the 13 rules drawn up for the 1774 tournament form the basis of the golf that is played to this day.

Leith Links

Continuing along Constitution Street past the superb **Leith Assembly Rooms** ㊿ on the right, used mainly for private parties and functions, the road approaches **Leith Docks**, evolved from John Rennie's plan in the early 19th century. The Victoria Docks were built in 1851; the Albert Docks in 1869, and the Edinburgh Docks in 1881. The buildings of ★★ **Bernard Street** (51), with the **Old Leith Bank** at its centre, mostly date from the 1770s. A statue of Robert Burns faces Constitution Street. **Bernard Street Bridge**, which crosses the river on the western corner with the Shore, was originally the Lower Drawbridge forming the link with Commercial Street and dating from the early 19th century. It was rebuilt in the 1950s.

All around this area are attractive bars and restaurants. The Ship Restaurant, which sits on ★★ **The Shore**, is a former pleasure yacht which belonged to the Irish Guinness family. The Shore, which is the official starting point of the **Water of Leith Walkway** (*see route 6, page 38*), has been revitalised, and a pedestrianised area leads into the docks beside the recently refurbished Malmaison Hotel and the Scot FM radio headquarters.

The ★ **Signal Tower** (52), built in 1686, once had a two-storey timber windmill above its existing tower. At the time of the Napoleonic Wars it was converted to enable flag communication with ships on the Firth of Forth. On the far side of the Water of Leith is the ★ **Customs House**. Designed by Robert Reid, it dates from 1812 and, although not open to the public, it is currently an annex to the Museum of Antiquities. ★ **King's Landing** was where George IV stepped ashore on his celebrated visit to Edinburgh in 1822. **King's Wark** was built by James I in 1438, but burnt down two centuries later. Since then it has been rebuilt and restored four times after successive fires.

★ **Lamb's House** (53), a 17th-century merchant's house in Water Street, was where Mary Queen of Scots rested upon her return to Scottish soil in 1561. Being the most ancient surviving dwelling house in Leith, it has been restored by the National Trust for Scotland and currently serves as a day centre for Edinburgh & Leith Old People's Welfare Council.

To the west of Commercial Street are the Sands where pirates were hanged 'within the floddis mark'. The last such execution for piracy took place in 1823 when two foreigners expiated their crime on a gibbet erected opposite the foot of Constitution Street.

From Commercial Street, the coastal road runs alongside the shores of the Firth of Forth into the former fishing village of Newhaven, and the harbour at Granton, now a popular yachting centre, then onwards towards Cramond, passing through various small industrial estates.

Newhaven was built by James IV in the 16th century as a dockyard for his expanding navy. An innovative king, he was determined to create the largest ocean-going vessel of his age, and thus the *Great Michael* was constructed here, 240ft (73 metres) long, to carry 300 sailors, 1,000 soldiers and 120 gunners. Following the king's death at Flodden in 1513, the *Great Michael* was loaned to the French, and later sold.

Burns on Bernard Street

Lamb's House

Newhaven

Excursion 1

Cramond – Lauriston Castle – South Queensferry – the Forth Bridges – Inchcolm Abbey – Hopetoun House (10 miles/16km)

Lauriston Castle

This route is to the west of the city and begins by taking Queensferry Road at the west end of Princes Street. It takes in a castle and country houses, and includes the possibility of venturing into the Firth of Forth on a ferry bound for Inchcolm Abbey with a chance to see puffins, seals and dolphins, or, at low tide, walking out to Cramond Island.

Turn off Queensferry Road at Davidson's Mains to ★ **Lauriston Castle** (April to October, daily except Friday, 11am–5pm; November to March, Saturday and Sunday only, 2–4pm). This incorporates a 16th-century tower once owned by the Napiers of Merchiston. Various owners have since built on additions, and it is now held in trust by the City as a museum.

Those familiar with Muriel Spark's 1961 novel *The Prime of Miss Jean Brodie* (or the 1969 film version starring Maggie Smith) will recall the picnics enjoyed by the strong-minded schoolmistress and her girls at Cramond. A lovingly restored, 18th-century village on the estuary of the River Almond on the Firth of Forth, it is reached

Flotilla at Cramond

by turning right off Queensferry Road, beyond Davidson's Mains, or continuing past Lauriston Castle. The name originates from the Cumbric *Caer Amon* ('Fort on the Almond'). Cramond was the site of a Roman harbour station. Excavations carried out in the 1960s indicate that it came under the control of Septimius Severus, Roman emperor from AD193 to 211. The remains of a Roman bathhouse were unearthed in the 1970s close to ★ **Cramond Kirk**; the current cruciform church dates from 1656, but the site was probably used by the early Christians.

Medieval Cramond came under the control of the bishops of Dunkeld who had their summer palace at **Cramond Tower**, a small, four-storey keep, restored during the 1980s. In 1680, the Inglis family began to build Cramond House which was completed in the following centuries, although half the village was demolished in the process. ★ **Cramond Inn** is today a popular restaurant and bar.

Cramond Tower

In the 18th century, there were four iron mills along the River Almond, and the first commercially produced Scottish crude steel came from Cramond. Today the village has become a popular summer yachting resort with a lively social life.

Since 1556 there has been a tiny ferry crossing to the **Dalmeny Estate** opposite, and at the **Cramond Brig** upstream, 'Jock' Howieson rescued from thieves 'the gudeman of Ballangeich', otherwise James V, who was in the habit of roaming around the countryside disguised as a traveller.

From the point, at low tide, it is possible to walk across the causeway to ★ **Cramond Island**, although it is essential to take note of the incoming tide times if you wish to avoid being stranded.

At the Barnton Roundabout on the Queensferry Road, the A90 leads to the ★★★ **Forth Road Bridge**. Turn off towards South Queensferry, and the road leads past the gates of ★★ **Dalmeny House**, home of the earls of Roseberry (July and August, Monday and Tuesday noon–5.30pm, Sunday 1–5.30pm). Designed in 1815 by William Wilkins, an English architect, it was the first Tudor Gothic revival house in Scotland.

The Primrose family acquired the estate, and Barnbougle Castle, a Norman keep situated on the shores of the Firth of Forth, in 1662. The story goes that the 3rd Earl,

'Maid of the Forth' with the Forth Road Bridge in the background

when rising from dinner at Barnbougle, was bowled over by a large wave of water and decided at once to build a larger, safer residence. The 5th Earl, Lord Rosebery, who was British prime minister in 1894–95, married a Rothschild heiress, and many of the treasures on display at Dalmeny come from their home at Mentmore, in England, sold in 1977. These include colourful tapestries designed by Goya for the Spanish royal residences, a selection of fine French furniture, and a Napoleon Room which is filled with the 5th Earl's collection of memorabilia belonging to the Emperor.

The town of **South Queensferry** crouches under the shadow of the ★★ **Forth Railway Bridge**, completed in 1890, with a total length over water of 6,156ft (1,876 metres). It opened up the east coast rail line to Perth, Inverness and Aberdeen. The ★★ **Queensferry Museum** (Monday, Thursday, Friday, Saturday 10am–1pm, 2.15–5pm; Sundays noon–5pm) at 53 High Street tells the story of the place and its people. The town was originally known as 'the Queen's Ferry' in honour of the saintly Queen Margaret, wife of Malcolm Canmore, who encouraged pilgrims in the 11th century to use the ferry crossing to visit the shrine of St Andrew in Fife by granting them free passage. The ★ **Hawes Inn**, which dates from 1683, was used by Robert Louis Stevenson in *Kidnapped* to accommodate the fictional meeting between Uncle Ebenezer and the Captain of the brig *Covenant*.

From the Hawes Pier, it is possible to take a cruise downriver on the ★★ ***Maid of the Forth*** (tel: 0131-331 4857 for sailing times) to the island of Inchcolm,where you can visit the ruin of **St Colm's Abbey** (founded in 1123), which gets a mention in Shakespeare's *Macbeth*. Seals and dolphins are to be seen en route, along with puffins, oyster catchers, cormorants and fulmars.

To the west of the town is ★★★ **Hopetoun House** (Easter to September daily 10am–5.30pm), the historic family home of the earls and marquesses of Linlithgow. The first house was designed by Sir William Bruce and built between 1699 and 1702. In 1721, William Adam was engaged to enlarge the mansion, and after his death the work was continued by his sons John, Robert and James. Most of the original 18th-century furniture and wall-coverings can be seen. The large, delighful grounds are full of rare specimen trees, and magnificent views of the Forth bridges can be enjoyed from the rooftop. Permanent exhibitions within the grounds include 'The Building of Hopetoun', 'Horse and Man in Scotland', and 'Wildlife', a seasonal display of specific interest to children. Visitors can wander at leisure in the magnificent parkland and enjoy the woodland walks. There is a Red Deer Park and nature trails. A countryside Ranger is in attendance.

The Forth Railway Bridge

Echoes of 'Kidnapped'

Hopetoun House

Musselburgh

Excursion 2

Musselburgh – Gullane – North Berwick (21 miles/ 34 km) *(see map on pages 46–47)*

This is the longest excursion. It begins at London Road, off Leith Walk, at the east end of Princes Street, and runs east of the city, largely following the coast to North Berwick. It passes through attractive small towns and villages and takes in a castle, several country estates and museums of motoring, mining, and golf.

Playing at Portobello

London Road leads past the 15,000-seater **Meadowbank Sports Stadium** erected for the Commonwealth Games of 1970. The road travels on to **Portobello** which reputedly was given its name by a seafarer who had taken part in the capture of Puerto Bello in Panama in 1739. It acquired burgh status on being amalgamated with Edinburgh in 1896, and by then it had become a popular residential and holiday resort. Sir Harry Lauder, the great music hall star of the early 20th century, was born is a cottage here in 1870, the son of a potter. In an attempt to restore Portobello's declining seaside appeal, large quantities of sand have been imported to improve the beach areas.

Musselburgh, at the mouth of the River Esk, was named after a bank of mussels in the 13th century. Its reputation as 'the Honest Toun' was earned when the inhabitants rejected a reward for honouring the body of the Earl of Moray, who died here in 1332. Flat and national hunt racing takes place regularly on **Musselburgh Racecourse** on the outskirts of the town as the road travels around the coast towards Prestonpans.

A hermitage and chapel dedicated to Our Lady of Loretto dates from the early 16th century, and was a place of pilgrimage for the sick. The name was taken by **Loretto School**, which has its grounds and houses within the town. One of these, **Pinkie House**, dates from the 16th century. Nearby is **Newhailes House**, the home of Lord Hailes at the time of Dr Samuel Johnson's 1773 tour of Scotland. Adjoining **Inveresk** is a pretty village of garden dwellings which has been conserved through the efforts of the Inveresk Preservation Society, and the National Trust for Scotland, which opens the gardens of ★★ **Inveresk Lodge** (Monday to Friday 10am–4.30pm, Saturday and Sunday 2–5pm; closed Saturday October to March).

Inveresk Lodge

Port Seton

On the A1 along the coast, there are numerous small towns and attractive villages to explore. At **Prestonpans** in the 12th century monks from Newbattle Abbey founded a salt-panning industry. The National Trust for Scotland has restored **Hamilton House**, built in 1628 for Sir John Hamilton, brother of the 1st Earl of Haddington.

One and a half miles to the southwest is a former colliery site with 800 years of mining history, now turned into the ★★**Prestongrange Industrial Heritage Museum** (March to October 11am–4pm). The Visitor Centre provides audio-visual programmes plus a walk-through exhibition. There is also a tea room and gift shop.

East of the town, a cairn commemorates the Battle of Prestonpans, a famous Jacobite victory won by Prince Charles Edward Stuart in 1745 against General John Cope and his government troops. Nearby **Cockenzie**, formerly a thriving fishing village, is dominated by an electricity-generating station. Adjacent **Port Seton** is noted as a summer holiday resort with an attractive beach, camping facilities, and safe bathing.

Further east and inland, **Haddington** was once described as the 'metropolus' of East Lothian. A royal burgh from the reign of David I, it was constantly attacked by invading English armies. The magnificent parish church of ★★ **St Mary the Virgin** stands away from the town centre overlooking the River Tyne, and has been superbly restored. The medieval burial aisle of the Maitlands of Lethington recalls the time when John Maitland, 1st Duke of Lauderdale, Charles II's commissioner, lived nearby. Believed to have been the birthplace of John Knox, Haddington was certainly the birthplace of Thomas Carlyle's wife Jane Welsh, and Samuel Smiles, the Victorian exponent of 'self-help'. ★★★ **Jane Welsh Carlyle's House** (Wednesday to Saturday 2–5pm) has been beautifully restored as a period home to reflect her life and times.

Jane Welsh Carlyle's House

Three miles (5km) to the south is **Bolton**, a picturesque village notable for the church in which are buried the mother, sister and brother of Robert Burns. Gilbert Burns,

Robert's brother, was factor to a nearby estate. Unlike his brother he was described as a man 'whose temperance and frugality were all that could be desired.'

Lennoxlove House

★★★ **Lennoxlove House** (Easter to October, Wednesday, most Saturdays, Sunday 2–4.30pm), 2 miles (3km) away, was formerly called Lethington and the home of William Maitland, Mary Queen of Scots' secretary, and his descendant, the Duke of Lauderdale. In 1682, the house was sold to Charles Stewart, Duke of Richmond and Lennox, and the name-change to Lennoxlove commemorates Frances 'La Belle Stuart', the doctor's daughter who became a mistress of Charles II. To the annoyance of Charles, she eloped with and married the Duke. When Lord Blantyre acquired the estate in the 18th century, it became Lennoxlove. It is now the home of the Duke of Hamilton and Brandon, housing many of the treasures from Hamilton Palace which was demolished in 1947. Among these are the death mask of Mary, Queen of Scots, and the silver casket in which she kept her letters.

Myreton Motor Museum

Back on the coastal route, **Aberlady** was once the port of Haddington, but the bay became silted over. A mile onwards, a small trestle bridge over the Peffer Burn leads to **Aberlady Bay Nature Reserve**, notable for its colony of pink-footed geese. Sunbathers who wish to make use of the dunes of this wide, sandy beach should note that the west end may be closed off to protect nesting terns.

Northeast is **Luffness House**, privately owned by the Hope family. Nearby is the **Myreton Motor Museum** (Easter to October, daily 10am–6pm; October to March, daily 10am–5pm), which accommodates vintage cars, commercial vehicles and bicycles. **Gosford House** (June and July, Saturday, Sunday and Wednesday 2–5pm) to the southwest of Aberlady, was built by Robert Adam and is the imposing home of the earls of Wemyss & March.

Golfing at Gullane

Next stop on the A188 is **Gullane**, a famous golfing village with three of its own 18-hole courses adjoining the Luffness Course to the south. To the east is the championship course of **Muirfield**, regularly home of the British Open Championship. The **Heritage of Golf Museum** (viewing by arrangement, tel: 01875-870277) on West Links Road, tells the story of golf from its arrival in Scotland from Holland in the 15th century.

Dirleton is an attractive village where houses, a 17th century church, and the Open Arms Hotel front onto a green across from the ruins of **Dirleton Castle** (April to September, daily 9.30am–6.30pm; October to March, Monday to Saturday 9.30am–4.30pm, Sunday 2–4pm), built by the Norman de Vaux family in 1225. In the grounds is a 17th-century bowling green and a dovecot dating from the same period. In 1650 the castle was virtually destroyed by General Monk and his Commonwealth artillery.

North Berwick

All along this coastline there are fine sandy beaches, notably Yellowcraigs. The seaside town of **North Berwick** sprang up on a promontory between two sheltered, sandy bays and prospered as a fishing port. It was incorporated as a royal burgh by Robert III, and is dominated by **North Berwick Law**, a mound rising to 613 ft (187 metres) above sea level. On the summit can be seen the jaw bones of a whale. In 1591, witches were brought to trial for plotting against James VI when he sailed over the North Sea to marry Anne of Denmark. The witches claimed they had been incited by the devil, appearing in the guise of the Earl of Bothwell. Bothwell was imprisoned, but escaped. The witches met a more unpleasant fate. Today this pretty seaside town is a yachting resort which relies mainly on tourism, although there is a certain retirement population. The **North Berwick Museum** (April to October 11am–5pm), in School Road, has galleries devoted to natural history, archaeology and the life of the town.

Bass Rock

Offshore is the **Bass Rock**, which rises 312ft (95 metres) above the sea. Half-way up the rock are the ruins of St Baldred's Chapel, named after an 8th-century hermit. Jacobite and other prisoners were held here over the centuries, but today is it a bird sanctuary providing a rare nesting colony for gannets. Boat trips from North Berwick Harbour can be made by arrangement.

East of the town as the A198 runs to meet the A1 to Dunbar, are the 14th-century ruins of **Tantallon Castle** (April to September, daily 9.30am–6.30pm; October to March, Monday to Wednesday and Saturday 9.30am–4.30pm, Thursday 9.30am–12.30pm, Sunday 2–4.30pm, closed Friday), formidable fortress of the Douglas Family. The walls are 14ft (4.3 metres) thick, and the well drops 100ft (30 metres) into rock. It was once considered the most impregnable castle in Scotland and for the sake of law and order was dismantled in the 18th century.

Tantallon Castle

Excursion 3

To Corstorphine, Ingliston and Edinburgh airport and on to Linlithgow Palace (15 miles/24 km) *(see map on pages 46–47)*

This route runs due west of Edinburgh to Linlithgow, taking in the zoo and agricultural museum, and finishing at Linlithgow Palace. Until the Edinburgh by-pass was built, this was the main route out of Edinburgh towards Stirling and Glasgow.

Zoo attraction

At **Murrayfield** is the Scottish Rugby Union's international stadium, and the adjoining ice rink is popular with curling clubs. Situated in 70 acres (28 hectares) of landscaped hillside is **Edinburgh Zoo** (April to September, Monday to Saturday 9am–6pm, Sunday 9.30am–6pm; October to March, Monday to Saturday 9am–5pm, Sunday 9.30am–5pm; November, December, January, Monday to Saturday 9am–4.30pm, Sunday 9.30am–4.30pm). The zoo, Britain's second largest, includes tigers, chimpanzees, giraffes and rhino. The Antarctic penguins here are the largest self-sustained colony in a zoo anywhere in the world and parade every day from April to September at 2pm (from October to March, weather permitting).

The village of **Corstorphine**, encroached upon by indifferent housing schemes, has a 15th-century collegiate church with pre-Reformation tombs. The name, first recorded in the 12th century, is derived from 'Torfinn's Crossing', after Thorfinn, the Viking prince who possibly did a power-sharing deal with Macbeth in the 11th century. **Corstorphine Hill**, which rises 530ft (162 metres), features **Clermiston Tower**, built in 1871 to mark the centenary of Sir Walter Scott's birth. In the village, there is a 17th-century circular dovecot close to the 55-ft (17-metre) high **Corstorphine Sycamore**, a botanical subspecies. The 'White Lady of Corstorphine', said to be the ghostly mistress of a 17th-century local landowner, is sometimes seen to turn about the tree. Close by is the **Doocot Tapestry Studios** (the Edinburgh Tapestry Workshop), founded by the 4th Marquess of Bute and inspired by William Morris and the early 20th-century Arts and Crafts Movement.

The Corstorphine Sycamore

Doocot Tapestry Studios

At the Maybury Roundabout is the **Maybury Conference and Banqueting Centre**, a classic example of art-deco architecture from the 1930s. Here the road divides to the right towards Barnton, in the middle being the old Turnhouse Airport road, and ahead, the A8 towards the Edinburgh by-pass roundabout at Gogar, the Royal Highland Showground, **Edinburgh Airport**, and the **Newbridge Roundabout** which leads onto the M8 and M9.

Ingliston, the parkland to the left of the A8, is the home of the annual **Royal Highland Show**. This June event is run by the Royal Highland and Agricultural Society, which acquired the estate, with **Ingliston House** serving as its headquarters, in 1958. ★★ **The Scottish Agricultural Museum** (April to September, daily 10am–5pm; October to March, Monday to Friday 10am–5pm) includes the oldest water driven mill in Scotland and has an audio-visual display. Regular weekend events at Ingliston throughout the year include motor racing and car boot sales. The location close to the Gogar Roundabout enables easy access from Glasgow, Stirling and the Forth Bridge.

Agricultural antiquity

Taking the M9 to **Stirling**, the road passes **Niddry Castle**, hard on the Edinburgh to Glasgow railway line. It was here in 1568 that Mary Queen of Scots fled following her escape from imprisonment at Loch Leven Castle. A few miles on, ★★★ **Linlithgow Palace** (April to September, daily 9.30am–6.30pm; October to March, Monday to Saturday 9.30am–4.30pm, Sunday 2–4pm) rises on the left-hand side of the motorway, in a spectacular setting behind Linlithgow Loch.

Linlithgow Palace

Linlithgow is a royal burgh, and many of the buildings have been restored by the National Trust for Scotland, then sold on to private owners. **St Michael's Parish Church**, close to the palace and dating from the 15th century, is listed as one of the finest medieval churches in Scotland. Edward I of England used Linlithgow as a base for his attack on Stirling, but the English garrison was taken by Scottish soldiers smuggled inside the walls in a hay waggon. The ★★ **Canal Museum** (Saturday and Sunday 2–5pm, during the week by appointment, tel: 01506-843194) houses records, photographs and relics relating to the Union Canal, correctly titled the Edinburgh & Glasgow Canal, which officially closed in 1965. This connected Edinburgh with Lock 16 of the Forth & Clyde Canal at Falkirk, making it possible to sail through to Glasgow. Arrangements can still be made for boat trips.

James I first built a palace here in 1425. His grandson and great-grandson made additions, and James V was born here in 1512. In 1542 Mary Queen of Scots was also born here, and the future Charles I was brought up at Linlithgow with his brother and sister, before his father inherited the throne of England and the family moved to London. Charles returned briefly in 1633, and Oliver Cromwell wintered here during his 1650 punitive trip to Scotland. After that the palace was largely abandoned until, almost a century after Cromwell's visit, it was set on fire following Prince Charles Edward Stuart's retreat from England. Although the damage remains to this day, the palace has been made safe for opening to the public.

Mary Queen of Scots

Liberton Parish Church

Excursion 4

Rosslyn Chapel – the Braid Hills (7 miles/11 km) *(see map on pages 46–47)*

This excursion due south of the city begins by crossing North Bridge at the east end of Princes Street and heads to the Braid Hills and Roslin.

From North Bridge the road travels through the university and residential districts collectively known as the **South Side**. To the southeast is **Liberton**, a 'village' on a hill with a fine parish church. The University of Edinburgh has its school of agriculture and departments of applied mathematics, engineering and genetics here. The **Edinburgh Computing Centre** is at King's Buildings on West Mains Road. The village's name may be a corruption of Lepertown, after a leper hospital that once stood here.

Royal Observatory

★ **Blackford Hill** forms a 100-acre (40-hectare) country park along the Hermitage of Braid, an estate with a castellated mansion built in the 18th century. After it was purchased by the city in 1889, a section was given over to a golf course, and another to the ★★ **Royal Observatory**, which has a visitor centre (Monday to Saturday 10am–5pm, Sunday noon–5pm). The **Harrison Arch**, by Sydney Mitchell, honours a former Lord Provost of Edinburgh who secured public access to the hill.

The kitchen, Craigmillar Castle

Off the A68 is ★★ **Craigmillar Castle** (April to September, Monday to Saturday 9.30am–6.30pm, Sunday 2–6.30pm; October to March, Monday to Wednesday and Saturday 9.30am–4.30pm, Thursday 9.30am–12.30pm, Sunday 2–4.30pm). Sited between Duddingston and Liberton, this is one of Scotland's most impressive medieval ruins. Although in existence in some form or other before 1212, the present L-plan tower dates from the late

15th century, and it was here, in 1566, that Mary Queen of Scots fled after the murder of David Rizzio, her private secretary, at the Palace of Holyroodhouse. Later that same year, a selection of Scottish noblemen are said to have met and plotted the murder of Lord Darnley, the Queen's husband.

Through Loanhead, a diversion leads onto the northern slopes of the **Pentland Hills** and the **Hillend Ski Centre**, Europe's longest artificial ski slope which is open all the year round. At night, when the slope is lit up against the dark sky, it is sometimes said to resemble 'a stairway to God'.

Following the A701 towards Penicuik, a turn to the left leads to Roslin, a mining village on the banks of the River North Esk. Beyond is **Rosslyn Castle**, which was built by Henry Sinclair, Earl of Orkney in the 14th century. The castle drops down the cliff-face of a rocky promontory which loops around the castle on three sides. Extensions in the 15th century included a deep gorge cut across the access side. This was given a drawbridge, later replaced by a bridge. The castle, currently owned by the Earl of Rosslyn, who is descended from the earls of Orkney, is administered by the Landmark Trust.

★★★ **Rosslyn Chapel** (Monday to Saturday 10am–5pm, Sunday noon–5pm or 4pm in winter), also known as the Collegiate Church of St Michael, was constructed in 1447, a short distance from the castle. The interior is decorated with remarkable carvings, notably the elaborately carved columns decorated with flowers showing the Cardinal Virtues and Seven Deadly Sins. The **Apprentice Pillar** is so called, the story has it, because it was carved by an apprentice stone-mason while the master mason was absent. So jealous was the older man on seeing the pillar that he killed the apprentice with a mallet. There is a legend, recalled in Sir Walter Scott's *Marmion*, that Knights of the Templar Order who fled to Scotland from Europe during the 12th-century reign of David I, are buried in full armour beneath the chapel. Another legend is that it was Prince Henry St Clair who set off from Orkney on a sea voyage, landing in Newfoundland and Nova Scotia where, guided by the Mic Mac Indians, he discovered America a century or so before Christopher Columbus. Carvings of American corn, unknown in Britain before the 16th century, feature in the frieze of the chapel.

From Roslin, the A701 runs south towards Peebles and Broughton. There are fine walks to be enjoyed in the **Braid Hills** which encroach on the Pentland Hills and reach across the city from Comiston to Liberton with a maximum height of 675ft (206 metres). Not without reason did invading armies of long ago survey the city from this vantage point.

The Apprentice Pillar, inside Rosslyn Chapel

Foxglove in the Braid Hills

Excursion 5

Colinton – Currie – Balerno – Threipmuir Reservoir (10 miles/16 km) *(see map on pages 46–47)*

Morningside's 'Holy Corner'

Craighouse

Drawing inside the Colinton Tunnel

This excursion to the southwest of the city is a rural ride up into the Pentland Hills. One of the more popular residential districts of Edinburgh is **Morningside**, celebrated for its refined variation of the Scottish accent, much emulated by Scottish comics. Situated on the south side of the city, Morningside is fringed by the **Grange**, **Merchiston**, **Craiglockhart** and **Comiston**. Where Colinton Road meets the Burghmuirhead, which is known as 'Holy Corner', four churches, one on each corner, welcome you. On Colinton Road, George Watson's College, Scotland's largest co-educational establishment, was started with a legacy bequeathed to 'endow a hospital for the maintenance of sons and grandsons of decayed merchants'.

Craiglockhart, to the southwest, was evolved in the early 20th century as another residential dormitory of fine villas. **Craighouse**, whose bulk dominates the surroundings, was formerly part of the Royal Infirmary, but has now been acquired by the University of Edinburgh.

Colinton began as a milling settlement tucked into a sandstone gorge formed by the Water of Leith. For those following the Water of Leith Walkway, **Colinton Tunnel** by-passes the village. It is dimly lit, but on the wall a drawing of a Balerno Pug, the small engine designed especially for the steep sided Colinton dell, can be discerned.

On reaching a stairway which leads to the footbridge, it is possible to take one of two routes. Following the old railway line, the path turns onto the north bank of the river and links up with the Union Canal towpath which goes northeast into Edinburgh. There's a picturesque riverside walk on the south bank.

The first traces of a village at Colinton appeared in 1095 when a ford across the river was an important crossing point over the steep river valley. Colinton means 'village in the wood' and during the 18th and 19th centuries was a centre for milling.

On 28 November 1666 the Covenanting Army which had risen up in defiance of Charles II's imposition of the Episcopalian religion on Scotland, were roundly defeated by General Tam Dalyell of the Binns at **Rullion Green**, not far away in the **Pentland Hills**. The **Covenanters' Monument** stands near Redford House, which is now integrated into the British army installation of **Redford Barracks** and **Greghorn Camp**.

Colinton House, which is now **Merchiston Castle School**, was built by Thomas Harrison for Sir William Forbes of Pitsligo in 1806. A high road above the dell leads to **Bonington Tower**, on the Pentland Slopes, once the home of Henry Cockburn, the great Scottish diarist. The road into the dell leads past various fine mansion houses.

On the far side of Colinton, the road connects with the A70 **Lanark Road**. **Juniper Green**, now submerged in a suburban sprawl, is a former grain, paper and snuff milling settlement on the Water of Leith. Woodhall House dates from the 16th century and the estate was purchased by Adam Cunyngham in 1629. At a later date, Charles I gave him the 'Supreme Commission to Punishing Receivers of Jesuits and Hearers of Mass'. Ironically, in 1961, the house was purchased by an English Jesuit Order.

Kinleith Mill was the largest mill on this section of the Water of Leith and produced 'featherweight paper' for export. The mill closed in 1966, and the area has been developed as Kinleith Industrial Estate. Moving on through the hamlet of Blinkbonny, created to house workers at the Kinleith Mill, the river passes through **Poet's Glen**, named for Robert Burns's friend and fellow-poet James Thomson who lived at the top of the glen.

Currie owes its origins to the farming community which surrounded it, taking its name from the Celtic *curagh* (a hollow), or from the Roman *coria* (a meeting place). Certainly, there were Roman forts in the area.

It is claimed that **Currie Bridge** is over 600 years old, and it unites the two halves of the village. The present Currie Kirk dates from 1784 and has stones of the Knights Templar in its graveyard. The sundial in front of the kirk was designed by a village schoolmaster and provides the times in various parts of the world.

Currie Bridge sundial

Situated in the grounds of the privately-owned Lymphoy House is the 15th-century **Lennox Tower**, with walls 7ft (2 metres) thick. A legend suggests that underground passages link it with Colinton.

Balerno

Balerno is on the highest workable stretch of the Water of Leith before it disappears up towards its source in the Pentland Hills. Its name is said to derive from *byrney* (a well-sheltered place). The locality is certainly sheltered, encouraging the cultivation of local gardens such as the **Balerno High School Garden**, developed by local residents and pupils. There has been a house at ★★ **Malleny**, on the Bavelaw Burn, a tributary of the Water of Leith, since the 15th century. The grounds of the present mansion, built in the early 17th century, are open to the public (April to October, daily 9.30am–7pm; November to March, daily 9.30am–4pm).

Walkers by Thriepmuir Reservoir

The side road leading to **Bavelaw Castle**, a 17th-century tower modernised by Sir Robert Lorimer, also leads to **Harlaw Reservoir** and **Thriepmuir Reservoir**, popular venues for country walks.

THE BALMORAL

Architecture

Opposite: Balmoral Hotel

One of the greatest achievements of the Scottish Enlightenment was the creation of Edinburgh's New Town, complimenting the narrow, fascinating streets of the medieval city. This architectural masterpiece was the result of a competition held in 1767 and won by James Craig, a 22-year-old architect.

Mid-18th century Edinburgh was a cramped, squalid place, quite unsuited to the ambitions of its citizens. It was hardly surprising, therefore, that George Drummond, six times Lord Provost, and his magistrates of Scotland's capital should decide to expand into 'the fields to the north', the land across the North Loch which lay in front of the castle rock.

Charlotte Square

Craig came up with the solution, and within his grid system was created the largest and finest show-place of Georgian-style architecture next to Bath. Influenced by the Palladian style of architecture, William Adam (1684–1748), and his sons Robert (1728–92) and James (1732–94), among others, began designing the classical squares and crescents of the first New Town, which evolved up to 1791.The second New Town was laid out to the north of the first, on the steep slope towards the Water of Leith, by Robert Reid (1774–1856). This concentrated on Great King Street, leading to Royal Circus, designed by William Playfair (1790–1857).

Westwards, the Moray Estate, with the 12-sided Moray Place, was completed on an interlinking system by James Gillespie Graham (1776–1885).

Chandelier in the Assembly Rooms

The early 20th century produced very little in Edinburgh that can be commended for architectural design, and the impatient desire for change prevalent after the end of World War II in 1945 caused civic vandalism to run rife throughout Britain's cities. Following a plan of 1948, Princes Street was to be completely re-built with a continuous covered walkway bridged at first-floor level. The concept was abandoned in 1978 – but not before much of the street had been pulled down and rebuilt.

St Mary's Episcopal Church

Happily, through the creation of preservation bodies such as the New Town Conservation Trust, the Cockburn Society, and a strict building policy adopted by the city authorities, the New Town has remained mostly intact. That's not to say that there haven't been more recent additions to Edinburgh's architectural heritage of which its citizens can be justifiably proud. Notably these include the 1991 Saltire Court (*see page 9*) by Campbell and Arnott, the 1994 glass-fronted Edinburgh Festival Theatre (*see page 27*) by architects Law Dunbar-Nasmith, and the 1995 Edinburgh International Conference Centre (*see page 33*), by Terry Farrell.

Literature

Edinburgh has inspired more than its fair share of literary figures, whether they have been simply visitors such as Daniel Defoe, or native sons and daughters.

The Scottish poet Robert Fergusson (1750–74) didn't have much of a chance to enjoy fame. Employed as a commissary's clerk, he contributed to *Ruddiman's Weekly Magazine,* which brought him local success but little money, and he died insane and impoverished in 1774. Fourteen years later his admirer, Robert Burns, paid for a headstone to be placed on his grave in Canongate Churchyard, and on the same spot in 1987 the Saltire Society (*see page 22*) erected its own tribute to Scotland's three Roberts, Fergusson, Burns and Stevenson.

Burns by Alexander Nasmyth

Robert Burns (1759–96) arrived in Scotland's Capital in 1786, aged 27. Having published the Kilmarnock edition of his poems, he was lionized overnight, but two years later abandoned 'Edina! Scotia's darling Seat!' for marriage to his childhood sweetheart, Jean Armour, and a farmhouse in Dumfries. His all too brief sojourn to the capital, however, had its impact and, apart from a monument at the foot of Calton Hill (*see page 30*) and a statue in Leith (*see page 45*), papers and relics are held in the Writers' Museum at Riddle's Court (*see page 15*)

James Boswell (1740–95) was born in Edinburgh, the son of Lord Auchinleck, a Court of Session judge. A precocious youth, he ran away to London when he was 18 and struck up a friendship with the elder Dr Johnson, whom he idolised and later immortalised with the famous biography published in 1791. On his European travels, through sheer brazen charm, he succeeded in introducing himself to Voltaire and Rousseau. Returning to Edinburgh, he married his cousin, Margaret Montgomerie, and was admitted to the Faculty of Advocates in 1773. He is best remembered for *Account of Corsica* and *The Journal of the Tour of the Hebrides.*

Sir Walter Scott by Raeburn

There are two literary giants which will always be synonymous with Edinburgh. The first, of course, is Sir Walter Scott (1771–1832); the second, Robert Louis Stevenson (1850–94).

Scott was born into middle-class Edinburgh, the son of a lawyer. As a teenager, he encountered Robert Burns in a New Town drawing room – a meeting of no significance to the celebrated bard but one which Scott would remember all his life. Following in his father's footsteps, Scott embarked on a career in the law which culminated with his becoming a sheriff (a judge in a local court). But, from an early age, writing was an obsession. Venturing into the deepest folds of the Scottish countryside,

The possibly apocryphal meeting between Burns and the young Walter Scott

he recorded the stories and oral tradition of the people of the land, which he saved for posterity through his prose and poems. This was his great achievement. Throughout his life his literary output, often urgently undertaken to pay off his creditors, was prodigious. Late at night, passers-by outside his home at 39 Castle Street would notice the candle-lit shadow of a quill pen being wielded strenuously.

Scotland owes a great debt to the Wizard of the North, as Scott was affectionately called, because, had he not penned such masterpieces as *The Border Minstrelsy*, *Marmion*, *The Lady of the Lake*, *Waverley*, *The Bride of Lammermoor* and *Ivanhoe*, those old tales would have probably been lost forever.

It was Scott who encouraged his contemporary James Hogg (1770–1835) who, having tended sheep in his youth, became known as 'The Ettrick Shepherd'. Although essentially a poet, his prose work *Private Memoirs and Confessions of a Justified Sinner*, with Edinburgh as it setting for much of the plot, remains by any standard a remarkable achievement.

Thomas de Quincey (1785–1859), the English author of *Confessions of an Opium Eater*, was lured to Edinburgh by the literary scene in 1828 and he lived and worked there until his death in 1859. His remains are interred in St Cuthbert's Kirkyard, behind Lothian Road.

Robert Louis Stevenson is buried in Samoa, where he died of tuberculosis. It had been a necessary exile, the Scottish climate being impossible for such an affliction, but he never lost his deep affection for his birthplace. From his birthplace at Howard Place, the Stevensons, a prominent family of lighthouse builders, moved to 17 Heriot Row. At Edinburgh University he studied engineering, then law, becoming an advocate in 1875. Thereafter he began to travel, selling his stories. In 1883, *Treasure Island*, inspired by the pond in the gardens in front of his childhood home,

Stevenson by Girolano Nerli

Sir Arthur Conan Doyle

brought him fame. *Kidnapped*, *Catriona*, and *The Master of Ballantrae* followed, but it is in his poetry and letters that Edinburgh appears again and again.

Stevenson stipulated that he did not wish to have a monument erected in his memory. There are memorials to him in California, in Davos, Switzerland, where he visited, and in Samoa. In Princes Street Gardens, Ian Hamilton Finlay has created a child's garden where a flagstone carries his initials (*see page 33*).

At Edinburgh University, Sir Arthur Conan Doyle (1859–1930), creator of the inscrutable literary detective Sherlock Holmes, was a contemporary of Stevenson. Born in 1858 in a now demolished tenement block near Piccardy Place, he began a career as a medical practitioner in Southsea, but before long turned to writing for a living. A statue of Sherlock Holmes mourning his creator by Gerald Ogilvy Laing stands on Picardy Place (*see page 29*).

Sir Compton Mackenzie (1883–1972), who wrote the classic *Whisky Galore* in 1947, moved to Edinburgh during the early 1960s and lived in Drummond Place. In the years before his death, he wrote the remarkable 10 octaves of his autobiography.

In recent years there has been no scarcity of literary output from Edinburgh. It is true to say, however, that this has largely been dominated by women, notably Edinburgh-born Muriel Spark, best known for *The Prime of Miss Jean Brodie*, and the romantic novels of Dorothy Dunnett, Mary Stewart, Joan Lingard and Alanna Knight.

Self-portrait, Sir Henry Raeburn

The Visual Arts

The fact that there are no less than 33 art galleries listed in central Edinburgh gives some indication as to the capital's status in the visual art world.

Following the genius of Allan Ramsay (1713–84), Sir Henry Raeburn (1756–1823) and Sir David Wilkie (1785–1841) in the 18th century, Edinburgh College of Art and the Royal Scottish Academy set about evolving a distinctive painterly tradition. This came into its own in the late 19th century with the impressionist seascapes of William McTaggart (1866–1925). During the early part of the 20th century, it was embraced by the Edinburgh colourists S.J. Peploe (1871–1935), Francis Cadell (1883–1937), and J.D. Fergusson (1874–1961).

William McTaggart's 'Spring'

More recently, Sir William MacTaggart jnr (1903–83), Sir William Gillies (1898–1973), Anne Redpath (1895–1966), and Sir Robin Philipson (1916–1992) have added great integrity to Edinburgh's reputation for painting.

The three major galleries are the National Gallery of Scotland, off Princes Street at the Mound, the Scottish National Gallery of Modern Art in Belford Road, and the Scottish National Portrait Gallery in Queen Street.

The Edinburgh International Festival

The Edinburgh Festival was created in the aftermath of adversity. In the closing months of World War II, Edinburgh's Lord Provost, Sir John Falconer, came up with the concept of a great celebration of the arts which would play a role in the healing process between nations. At the same time, he believed such an event would re-establish Edinburgh as a European city of culture with a worldwide reputation. Before long, a chance encounter with Rudolph Bing, administrator of the Glyndebourne Festival Opera and himself a refugee from Nazi Europe, proved the catalyst.

Together they persuaded Edinburgh's naturally nervous city fathers – and more importantly a recently conceived British Arts Council – to put up the finance, and in August 1947 the curtain went up on the first Edinburgh Festival production. It was a resounding success and the word soon spread internationally that Edinburgh was the place to be – this despite Edinburgh's only licensed restaurant closing at 9pm.

In the years that followed, all the great orchestras began to arrive. Yehudi Menuhin, the great violinist, became almost an annual fixture. Joan Sutherland, Tito Gobbi, Elizabeth Schwarzkopf, Maria Callas and Placido Domingo came to sing, despite the absence of a respectable opera house. Margot Fonteyn and Rudolph Nureyev came to dance. As the main Festival grew, so did the Festival Fringe, with something like 500 companies spilling into every available performance space to present well over 1,000 shows in 10,000 performances.

Edinburgh adapted accordingly, with successive municipal authorities taking an increasingly liberal attitude towards closing times. As a result, for at least four weeks of the year, Edinburgh can be said to be open all night.

Today several festivals take place concurrently during the month of August. There's the Edinburgh International Festival itself (tel: 0131-473 2001), the Edinburgh Festival Fringe (tel: 0131-226 5257), the Edinburgh Film Festival (tel: 0131-228 4051), the Edinburgh Military Tattoo (tel: 0131-225 1188), the Edinburgh International Jazz Festival (tel: 0131-557 1642), and the Edinburgh Book Festival (tel: 0897-500 010). The climax each year comes with the spectacular open-air Scottish Chamber Orchestra Concert and firework display from Edinburgh Castle.

Edinburgh has always succeeded in presenting unique and unexpected events. As a festival, it embraces all the arts, and the achievements and reputation of early festivals ensured that there has never been a shortage of world-class companies willing to take part.

World-class performances

The Fringe's nerve centre

TRAVEL AGENCY
220-0100
A TASTE OF SCOTLAND
SCOTCH BROTH
NUTTY BROCCOLI & MUSHROOM BAKE
BEEF & VENISON PIE
LIVER & RED WINE
DIRTY DICKS
REAL ALE
GUEST ALES

Food and Drink

Opposite: Lunchtime jollity

Restaurants

Strongly influenced by the Scottish Tourist Board's Taste of Scotland initiative, most Edinburgh restaurants guarantee fresh Scottish seafood, game, beef and lamb, and organic vegetables. There are also a selection of French, Italian, Mexican, Indian and Chinese restaurants, and other ethnic eateries.

£££ expensive (over £50 for two); **££** moderate (£30–50 for two); **£** inexpensive (under £30 for two). Price brackets include house wine.

The Witchery by the Castle, 352, Castlehill, tel: 0131-225 5613. Atmospheric restaurant located next to the Castle, featuring traditional/new-wave Scottish cuisine. £££

Prestonfield House Hotel (Open 7 days), Priestfield Road, tel: 0131-668 3346. Superb ambiance in 17th-century mansion below Salisbury Crags. Classic Scottish/French cuisine. Outstanding wine cellar. £££

Haggis and neeps

The Vintners Room, The Vaults, 87, St Giles Street, Leith, tel: 0131-554 6767. Dine by candle-light on white linen tablecloths in the oldest commercial building in Scotland, once used by the monks of Holyrood. French provincial cuisine and cooked to order. £££

Another favourite: salmon 'n' chips

The Pompadour Restaurant at the Caledonian Hotel, Princes Street, tel: 0131-459 9988. French-influenced dishes and feminine grey/pink decor in honour of its namesake, Madam de Pompadour. Try finnan haddock cheesecake with caviar. £££

Raffaelli Restaurant (Monday to Friday),11, Randolph Place, tel: 0131-225 6060. Sumptuous Florentine decor in dark green complements the Northern Italian dishes. £££

Martins Restaurant 70, Rose Street North Lane, tel: 0131-225 3106, Central, but difficult to find being in a lane off the Rose Street pedestrian precinct. Excellent game, fish and organic vegetable dishes with Scottish and Irish farmhouse cheeses recommended. ££

Kellys, 46, West Richmond Street, tel: 0131-668 3847. Established family business with the emphasis on good, wholesome Scottish food. Intimate atmosphere. ££

Vito's Restaurant, 55, Frederick Street, tel: 0131-225 5052. Mainly recipes from southern Italy, with seafood a speciality. Closed Sunday November to April. ££

The Atrium, Cambridge Street, tel: 0131-228 8882. Simple yet elegant food. Chef Andrew Radford has won an international reputation in this post-modern style eatery attached to the Traverse Theatre. ££

Cosmo Restaurant, 58, North Castle Street, tel: 0131-226 6743. Popular for corporate entertaining because of intimate surroundings. Mussels cooked in their own juices with white wine and garlic are recommended. ££

Creelers Seafood Restaurant, 3, Hunter Square, tel: 0131-220 4447. With strong connections with the Isle of Arran. ££

Skippers Bistro, 1a Dock Place, Leith, tel: 0131-554 1018. Brasserie-style with atmosphere. Specialises in fish dishes. There is a 14-page wine list. ££

The Raj Restaurant, 89, Henderson Street, Leith, tel: 0131-553 3980. This spacious restaurant offers a waterfront view and Goan cuisine. Owner Tommy Miah runs a Curry Club and sells curry pastes if anybody wants to have a go at making their own. ££

Fresh fish for sale

(fitz)Henry's Restaurant, 19, Shore Place, Leith, tel: 0131-555 6625. Eccentric atmosphere with imaginative dishes and superb wine list. ££

The Shore Bar and Restaurant, 3–4, The Shore, Leith, tel: 0131-553 5080. Very popular bar and one-room restaurant. Menu changes daily. Strong bias towards fish dishes. £

Pierre Victoire, 10, Victoria Street, tel: 0131-225 1721 and at 8, Union Street, tel: 0131-557 8451. There are other branches too of this inexpensive French bistro. £

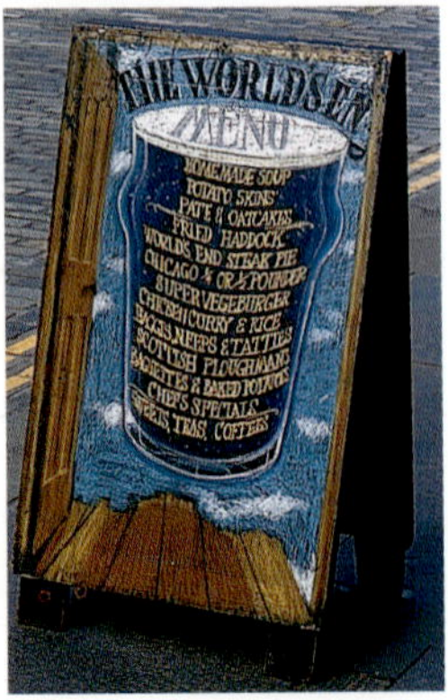

Royal Mile menu

Harry Ramsden's, Newhaven Fish Market, Newhaven Harbour, tel: 0131-551 5566. Fish and chips in a great waterfront location on the Firth of Forth. £

Henderson's Salad Table, 94, Hanover Street, tel: 0131-225 2131. Long-established, family-owned vegetarian restaurant. £

Maison Hector, 47, Deanhaugh Street, tel: 0131-332 5328. Trendy decor and simple, appealing dishes. £

Kweilin, 19, Dundas Street, tel: 0131-557 1875. Large space serving authentic Cantonese dishes; perhaps the best Chinese in town. £

Shopping

The Old Town

The Grassmarket has mostly been taken over by restaurants and bars, but Victoria Street offers an exceptional range of curio shopping with the Byzantium Market at the top featuring a range of craft stalls. **The Royal Mile** is mostly given over to souvenirs and tartan, but running off this is **Cockburn Street** for the trendy shopper, with such shop names as Whiplash Trash and Return to Sender.

The New Town

Princes Street remains Edinburgh's main shopping street with the predictable presence of Marks & Spencer, BHS, Debenhams, Aitken & Niven, Littlewoods, Boots, HMV, Virgin, and Waterstone's. Jenners is the only remaining independently-owned Princes Street department store.

Parallel streets such as the pedestrianised **Rose Street**, the larger **George Street**, and **Thistle Street** provide a range of smaller shops. **Stockbridge** and **Broughton Street** are good for antique hunters.

Antique shop, St Stephen Street

Specialist stores

• *Haggis:*
Macsween of Edinburgh, 118, Bruntsfield Place.
Crombies of Edinburgh, 97, Broughton Street.

• *Scotch whisky shops:*
Cadenheads Whisky Shop,172, Canongate.
Royal Mile Whiskies, 379–381, High Street.
The Whisky Shop, Waverley Shopping Centre.

• *Highland dress and tartan:*
Kinloch Anderson, Commercial Street/Dock Street, Leith, are kiltmakers to the Royal Family.
The Scotch House, 39–41 Princes Street.
Hector Russell Kiltmaker, 95, Princes Street, 137–141 High Street, and 509 Lawnmarket.
Geoffrey (Tailor) Kiltmakers, 57–59 High Street.
Hugh Macpherson (Scotland), 17 West Maitland Street.

• *Designer Scottish cashmere:*
Harrisons of Edinburgh, 24 Jane Street.
Belinda Robertson Cashmere, 22 Palmerston Place.

• *Scottish designer woollens:*
Bill Baber Knitwear Design, 66 Grassmarket.
Gleneagles of Scotland, Waverley Shopping Centre.
Number Two, 2 St Stephen Street.

• *Scottish jewellery:*
Hamilton & Inches, 87 George Street.
Joseph Bonnar, 72 Thistle Street.
Clarksons of Edinburgh, 87 West Bow.
Laing the Jeweller, 28 Frederick Street.
Mappin & Webb, 88 George Street.

A tranche of tartans

Nightlife

Edinburgh is transformed during the August festival, and bars and restaurants are granted special late licences. For the remainder of the year, the city's nightlife is more docile though many bars close at midnight or later, and clubs at about 3am. Details of current attractions at the city's dozen or so cinemas and theatres can be found in local newspapers or in *The List* magazine.

Catering for all thirsts

Bars

- *New Town*

The Abbotsford, 3 Rose Street, tel: 0131-225 5276. Round island bar and Victorian decor. The constantly changing ales are a house speciality.

The Baillie, 2 St Stephen's Street, tel: 0131-225 4673. Cosy, spacious island bar with mixed clientele.

The Café Royal Circle Bar, 17, West Register Street, tel: 0131-556 1884. A fine, tiled bar which attracts a large clientele from local office workers and visitors.

- *Old Town*

The Bow Bar, 80 West Bow, tel: 0131-226 7667. Twelve real ales and 135 malts – a connoisseur's heaven.

Deacon Brodie's Tavern, 435 Lawnmarket, tel: 0131-225 6531. A traditional Old Town Scottish bar.

Greyfriar's Bobby Bar, 34, Candlemaker Row, tel: 0131-225 8328. A student favourite.

Scruffy Murphy's, 49 George IV Bridge, tel: 0131-225 1681. There's live music at weekends in this Irish theme pub.

On the town

Nightclubs/Discotheques

Club Mercado, 36–39 Market Street, tel: 0131-226 4224. Young crowd. Friday nostalgia night until 3am.

The Citrus Club, 40–42 Grindlay Street, tel: 0131-622 7086. Student, Punk, '80s, and Funk.

The Minus One Club, Carlton Highland Hotel, North Bridge, tel: 0131-556 7277. For more mature patrons.

Honeycomb, 36–38A Blair Street, tel: 0131-220 4381. Designer chic, varied clientele.

The Subway, 6 Cowgate, tel: 0131-225 6766. Young and vibrant.

Jazz and Folk

Venues with regular jazz residencies include: **Cellar No.1**, Chamber Street (most nights; tel: 0131-220 4298) and **Henderson's**, 25 Thistle Street (Wednesday to Friday; tel: 0131-225 2605). Folk residencies are at: **Tron Ceilidh House**, 9 Hunter Square (most nights, tel: 0131-226 0931) and **Finnigan's Wake**, 9b Victoria Street (nightly; tel: 0131-226 3816).

Active Pursuits

Fishing

There are a number of well-stocked rivers and reservoirs within easy reach of the city and brown trout are to be found in the Water of Leith. Sea angling is available on the Firth of Forth. A booklet entitled *Freshwater Fishing in the Lothian Region* gives up-to-date information on angling opportunities, and is available from bookshops and tourist information centres.

The Scots invented it

Golf

An Edinburgh & Lothians Golf Pass (4 or 2 day) can be purchased from any Tourist Board Information Centre, or by telephoning 0131-558 1072. This gives access to 12 courses, of which five – Craigmillar, Liberton, Lothianburn, Swanston, and Torphin – are in the immediate city environs.

Municipal courses (open to all) are at Braid Hills (tel: 0131-447), Carrick Knowe (tel: 337 1096), Craigentinny (tel: 0131-554 7501), Portobello (nine holes; tel: 0131-669 4361) and Silverknowes (tel: 0131-336 3843).

Riding

Various out-of-town stables provide riding facilities and pony-trekking. These include:
Edinburgh & Lasswade Riding Centre, Lasswade, tel: 0131-663 7676.
The Trekking Centre, Windy Gowl Farm, Carlops, tel: 01968-661095.

Skating

Murrayfield Ice Rink is a popular venue for skaters throughout the year. Skates can be hired. Sessions in the afternoons, evenings and at weekends. For further information, tel: 0131-337 6933.

Skiing

Situated at Hillend Country Park, on the Biggar Road, half-an-hour by bus or car from the city centre, is the Hillend Ski Centre. Features include Europe's longest artificial ski slope, a triple lift system, an alpine lodge and restaurant, and equipment hire. Open daily 9.30am–9pm; closes at 7pm summer weekends. Tel: 0131-445 4433.

Swimming

Edinburgh has a superb swimming complex built for the 1970 Commonwealth Games. The Royal Commonwealth Pool is at Dalkeith Road, tel: 0131-667 7211. The City of Edinburgh Council has swim centres at Dalry, Glenogle, Infirmary Street, Leith, Portobello and Warrender.

Winging it

L785 FOV

Getting There

By car

Edinburgh is approached from the south by the A1 coastal road from Berwick Upon Tweed, the A68 from Jedburgh, and the A7 from Selkirk. There is no motorway route into the southeast of Scotland, but this is compensated for by the beauty of the countryside.

The M6, which travels up the west coast of England meets with the A74 north of Carlisle, which becomes the M74 and connects with the M8 northeast of Glasgow. Travelling east, the M8 meets with the Edinburgh City by pass, west of Edinburgh. The M8 also connects with the M9 from Stirling at the Newbridge Roundabout, northwest of the city.

From Perth, the M90 turns into the A90 before crossing the Forth Road Bridge and entering the city suburbs at Barnton.

By coach

There are daily and overnight long-distance bus services to St Andrew Square Bus Station from London and elsewhere in the UK. For details, contact: National Express, tel: 0870 5808080 (from the UK or abroad), or Scottish Citylink, tel: 0990 505050.

By train

Edinburgh Waverley and Edinburgh Haymarket stations service all incoming trains. For current fares and timetables, and also for credit card sales and reservations, tel: 0345-484950.

GNER InterCity operate regular hourly services between London Kings Cross and Edinburgh Waverley, 6am–7pm. The service, which on average takes under 5 hours, is popular and reservations are recommended.

The Freedom of Scotland Travel Pass from ScotRail gives unlimited travel on Scotland's rail network, and is available over 8 or 15 consecutive days.

By air

Edinburgh Airport, northwest of the city, on the Glasgow Road, is served by regular flights from London Heathrow, London Gatwick, Luton, Birmingham, East Midlands, Leeds/Bradford, Cardiff and Belfast.

Airport information: tel: 0131-333 1000; British Airways, tel: 0345 222111; British Midland, tel: 0131-334 3302/3; KLM Air UK, tel: 0131-344 3180; Servisair (for other airlines flying to Edinburgh) tel: 0131-344 3111.

Although there are currently no scheduled flights from North America, there are several regular flights to Prestwick and Glasgow.

Opposite: Moray Place

Not an easy ride

Regular services

Getting Around

The Tourist Information Centre is above the Waverley Shopping Centre at 3 Princes Street (tel: 0131-473 3800). Public transport information is available by calling freephone Traveline, tel: 0800 232323.

Car & bike rental

This is well worth doing if you want to explore the surrounding districts and countryside. Car firms include:
Arnold Clark, tel: 0131-228 4747/ 0131-458 1501.
Avis, tel: 0131-337 6363/0131-3331866.
Condor, tel: 0131-229 6333/0131-228 6000.
Hertz, tel: 0131-333 1019/0131-556 8311/0131-557 5272.
Melville's, tel: 0345 525354/0131-337 5333.
National Car Rental, tel: 0131-337 8686/0131-333 1922.

Bicycles can be hired from: Edinburgh Cycle Hire, 29 Blackfriars Street, tel: 0131-556 5560.

Pay as you enter

Buses

The main bus company is Lothian Region Transport (LRT), with maroon and white buses. You buy a ticket as you enter the bus (exact change required) and it is important not to lose it before you reach your destination as an inspector may want to see it. For details: LRT, Ticket Centre, Waverley Bridge, tel: 0131-556 6363. Timetables, fares and route information are posted at the main city centre bus stops.

50 minutes to Glasgow

Trains

Trains to and from Glasgow run on the hour and half-hour from Waverley and Haymarket Stations. The journey time is 50 minutes. ScotRail enquiries, tel: 0345-484950.

Taxis

Taxi ranks are located throughout the city centre, notably outside Waverley and Haymarket Stations, the Caledonian Hotel at the West End of Princes Street, and beside the Playhouse Theatre at the top of Leith Walk. Edinburgh's black cabs operate 24 hours. Taxi firms include: Central Radio Taxis, tel: 0131-229 2468; City Cabs, tel: 0131-228 1211; Radiocabs, tel: 0131-225 9000.

Car parks

At the east end of Princes Street, at the top of Leith Street, is the Greenside Car Park (tel: 558 3518) and the St James Centre (National Car Parks Ltd), tel: 556 5066. The Waverley Car Park is located at 6 New Street, behind Waverley Station (tel: 557 8526), and National Car Parks also operate a park at Castle Terrace, off Lothian Road (tel: 0131-229 2870).

Facts for the Visitor

Keeping in touch

Tourist Information

The Edinburgh & Scotland Tourist Information Centre (May, June, September, Monday to Saturday 9am–7pm, Sunday 11am–7pm; July, August, Monday to Saturday 9am–8pm, Sunday 11am–8pm; October to April, 9am–6pm, Sunday 11am–6pm) is located on top of the Waverley Shopping Centre at the east end of Princes Street. The staff can assist with accommodation, bookings, advance reservations, ticket sales and exclusive souvenirs, and there is a bureau de change facility. Tel: 0131-473 3800.

There is also a branch of this information desk (April to October, Monday to Saturday 8.30am–9.30pm, Sundays 9.30am–9.30pm; November to March, Monday to Friday 9am–6pm, Saturday and Sunday 9am–5pm) at Edinburgh Airport, tel: 0131-333 2167.

Travel services

American Express,139 Princes Street, tel: 0131- 225 7881; foreign exchange, tel: 0131-225 9179.
Thomas Cook, 26–28 Frederick Street, tel: 0131-465 7700.

Cash dispensers and Link machines

Abbey National: Hanover Street
Bank of Scotland: The Mound
Clydesdale Bank: George Street
Halifax: George Street
Lloyds: George Street
National Westminster: George Street
Nationwide: George Street
Royal Bank of Scotland: St Andrew Square

Sightseeing tours

The most popular guided tour is the open-top bus tour of the city which operates from Waverley Bridge. A variety of evening, on-foot guided excursions throughout the Old Town are also available. These include: Auld Reekie Tours, tel: 0131-557 4700; Mercat Tours, tel: 0131-661 4541; The Witchery Tours, tel: 0131-225 6745.

Postal services

The main post office customer service centre is at 10, Brunswick Road, tel: 0345 223344. City centre post offices are located in the St James Centre (east end of Princes Street), at 7 Hope Street and 40 Frederick Street.

Newspapers

Foreign visitors will find a comprehensive range of overseas newspapers and periodicals available at International Newsagents, 351 High Street, tel 0131-225 4827.

Ring for help

Emergencies

Police, ambulance, fire brigade: 999.
Lothian & Borders Police Headquarters, Fettes Avenue, tel: 0131-311 3131.
Royal Infirmary of Edinburgh, tel: 0131-536 1000.
Western General Hospital, tel: 0131-537 1000.

Lost and Found

Lost items are invariably handed in to police stations and passed to the Police Headquarters, Fettes Avenue, Edinburgh EH4 1RB, tel: 0131-311 3141. For belongings mislaid on public transport, the appropriate company should be contacted.
Waverley Railway Station, tel: 0131-556 2477.
Lothian Region Transport, tel: 0131-554 4494.
St Andrew Square Bus Station, tel: 0131-663 9233.

Disabled access

For a largely Georgian/Victorian city, Edinburgh is remarkably well equipped for those with disabilities, although public transport can be a problem. Many taxis carry a wheelchair symbol on the front.

With a few exceptions, however, most public buildings now have wheelchair facilities and there are rigid conditions for new building.

For further information contact Lothian Coalition of Disabled People, 57, Albion Road, tel: 0131-475 2360. For information on transport, tel: 0345 585641.

High Kirk of St Giles

Photography

In the majority of Edinburgh's museums, castles and art galleries, photography is not allowed. In some cases permission can be obtained, but flash photography is not encouraged.

Religion

- *Church of Scotland*

High Kirk of St Giles, High Street, tel: 0131-225 4363.
St Andrew's & St George's, George Street, tel: 0131-225 3847.

- *Scottish Episcopal*

St Mary's Cathedral, Palmerston Place, tel: 0131-225 6293.
St John's Church, Princes Street, tel: 0131-229 2978.

- *Roman Catholic*

St Mary's Cathedral, York Place, tel: 0131-556 1798.
St Patrick's Church, Cowgate, tel: 0131-556 1973.

- *Jewish*

Edinburgh Hebrew Congregation, 4, Salisbury Road, tel: 0131-667 3144.

- *Islam*

Central Mosque, 50, Potterow, tel: 0131-667 1777.

Spectator sports

● *Rugby*

Internationals are held between January and March at Murrayfield Stadium on Corstorphine Road under the auspices of the Scottish Rugby Union, tel: 0131-346 5000.

● *Football*

Edinburgh has two Premier Division clubs, Heart of Midlothian and Hibernian. Heart of Midlothian have their playing ground at Tynecastle, on Gorgie Road, at the west end of the city, and Hibernian play at Easter Road, north of London Road, at the east end. There are matches on Saturdays and Wednesdays throughout the season.

● *Horse Racing*

Twenty-two race meetings, Flat and National Hunt, are held every year at Musselburgh Racecourse, tel: 0131-665 2859. Meetings are usually held mid-week.

● *Highland Games*

Edinburgh Highland Games, featuring trials of strength, caber tossing, and tug-o-wars, take place throughout the summer at different city locations. For details, tel: 0131-319 2005.

Edinburgh for Children

Edinburgh goes so far as to publish a booklet entitled *Child Friendly Edinburgh* (available at tourist information centres) to emphasise how welcoming it is towards the younger generation. There are numerous children's play areas around the city.

During the summer, **Portobello Beach**, although its glamour has long faded for adults, makes for a diverting seaside excursion for children (*see page 50*).

Pick a penguin at the zoo

Edinburgh Zoo (*see page 54*) and **Deep Sea World**, over the Forth Road bridge at North Queensferry, are recommended diversions. The aquarium gives a diver's eye-view of the denizens of the deep.

The **Camera Obscura** at Outlook Tower, Castlehill, Royal Mile (*see page 15*) is popular with children. An enthralling 19th-century version of TV, it projects a moving picture of life outside onto a screen.

The **Museum of Childhood** in the Royal Mile (*see page 22*) is an intriguing visit, but for the more active child, the water-slides at Leith Waterworld (tel: 0131-555 6000) or flumes at the Royal Commonwealth Pool (tel: 0131-667 7211) are a real treat.

Toys were us

During the **Edinburgh Festival** the streets are full of jugglers and performance artists, and on Fringe Sunday in Holyrood Park there are side-shows and numerous distractions such as face-painting workshops. But be warned that the crowds can become exhausting.

Where to Stay

Advance booking is essential throughout the summer months, and particularly during August when the city can be filled to capacity and visitors have to be diverted to Stirling, Perth or Glasgow. Expect to pay higher prices during August. Out-of-season prices vary considerably.

The Edinburgh and Scotland Tourist Information Centre provides a room-finding service, tel: 0131-473 3800.

The Balmoral Hotel

Hotels

££££(over £170 per night double)

The Balmoral Hotel, 1, Princes Street, tel: 0131-556 2414. Imposing 5-Star hotel at east end of Edinburgh's main shopping street.

The Caledonian Hotel, Princes Street, tel: 0131-459 9988. Esteemed 5-Star Hotel at west end of Edinburgh's main shopping street.

The George Hotel Intercontinental, 19–21, George Street, tel: 0131-225 1251. Well situated in the heart of the New Town.

The Holiday Crown Plaza, 80 High Street, The Royal Mile, tel: 0131-557 9797. In appearance vernacular architecture, but in fact of recent construction.

The Howard Hotel, 32–36 Great King Street, tel: 0131-557 3500. Quiet, luxuriously decorated hotel in New Town. First-class basement restaurant.

The Sheraton Edinburgh Hotel, Festival Square, tel: 0131-229 9131. Five-star hotel in the heart of Edinburgh's financial and theatre district.

£££ (over £120 per night double)

The Carlton Highland Hotel, North Bridge, tel: 0131-472 3102. Good location at Edinburgh's east end, a step from the Royal Mile and Princes Street.

The Hilton National Hotel, 69 Belford Road, tel: 0131-332 2545. In walking distance from the city centre.

The Mount Royal Hotel, Princes Street, tel: 0131-225 7161. Central location with views of Edinburgh Castle.

The Royal Terrace Hotel, 18 Royal Terrace, tel: 0131-557 3222.

The Bank Hotel and, behind, the Holiday Crown Plaza

££ (over £60 per night double)

The Albany Hotel, 39–43 Albany Street, tel: 0131-556 0397. Comfortable, family-owned hotel with a good restaurant.

The Bank Hotel, 1 South Bridge, tel: 0131-556 9043. Unusual corner-building hotel with limited accommodation of 9 bedrooms in the very heart of the Old Town.

The Point Hotel, 34 Bread Street, tel: 0131-221 5555. Refurbished. Close to theatre and financial centre.

The Caledonian Hotel

£ (under £60 per night double)

The Apex International Hotel, Grassmarket, tel: 0131-300 3456. Refurbished Georgian building, on the spartan side. Central Old Town with views over the Castle.

Ivy Guest House, 7 Mayfield Gardens, tel:0131-667 3411. Family run; Tourist Board 2-Crown Commended.

Newington Guest House, 18 Newington Road, tel: 0131-667 3356. Family-run guest house with 8 bedrooms.

On the outskirts of Edinburgh:

£££

Norton House Hotel, Ingliston, tel: 0131-333 1275. Country house hotel close to Edinburgh airport.

The Royal Scot Hotel, 111 Glasgow Road, tel: 0131-334 9191. On main western approach into the city, near zoo.

££

Braid Hills Hotel, 134 Braid Road, tel: 0131-447 8888. Quiet.

Forte PostHouse Hotel, Corstorphine Road, tel: 0131-334 0390.

Malmaison Hotel, Tower Place, Leith, tel: 0131-468 5000. Superb renovation of former commercial building. Four-poster beds and a first-class restaurant.

Prestonfield House Hotel, Priestfield Road, tel: 0131-668 3346. Old-world charm with five bedrooms in 17th-century mansion located under Salisbury Crags.

Youth Hostels

Scottish Youth Hostels Association, 18, Eglinton Crescent, tel: 0131-337 1120.

Alternative cheap accommodation, available to everyone, can be booked out of term at Edinburgh University. Details from British Universities Accommodation Consortium, Box H9, University Park, Nottingham, NG7 2RD.

The Malmaison Hotel

Index